GENIUS
LOCI

CHRISTIAN
NORBERG-SCHULZ

GENIUS LOCI

TOWARDS A PHENOMENOLOGY OF ARCHITECTURE

RIZZOLI
NEW YORK

Design Diego Birelli
Layout Lucia Vigo
Editor Gabriella Borsano

Printed in Italy
First published in Italian
under the title "Genius loci - paesaggio, ambiente, architettura"
1979 © Copyright Gruppo Editoriale Electa - Milano

Published in the United States of America in 1980 by:

*R*IZZOLI INTERNATIONAL PUBLICATIONS, INC.
712 Fifth Avenue/New York 10019

Library of Congress Catalog Card Number: 79-56612
ISBN: 0-8478-0287-6

"Logic is doubtless unshakable,
but it cannot withstand
a man who wants to live."
Franz Kafka: *The Trial*

The present book forms a sequel to my theoretical works *Intentions in Architecture* (1963) and *Existence, Space and Architecture* (1971). It is also related to my historical study *Meaning in Western Architecture* (1975). Common to all of them is the view that architecture represents a means to give man an "existential foothold". My primary aim is therefore to investigate the *psychic* implications of architecture rather than its practical side, although I certainly admit that there exists an interrelationship between the two aspects. In *Intentions in Architecture* the practical, "functional", dimension was in fact discussed as part of a comprehensive system. At the same time, however, the book stressed that the "environment influences human beings, and this implies that the purpose of architecture transcends the definition given by early functionalism". A thorough discussion of perception and symbolization was therefore included, and it was emphasized that man cannot gain a foothold through scientific understanding alone. He needs *symbols*, that is, works of art which "represent life-situations". The conception of the work of art as a "concretization" of a life-situation is maintained in the present book. It is one of the basic needs of man to experience his life-situations as meaningful, and the purpose of the work of art is to "keep" and transmit meanings. The concept of "meaning"was also introduced in *Intentions in Architecture*. In general, the early book aimed at understanding architecture in *concrete* "architectural" terms, an aim which I still consider particularly important. Too much confusion is created today by those who talk about everything else when they discuss architecture! My writings therefore reflect a *belief* in architecture; I do not accept that architecture, vernacular or monumental, is a luxury or perhaps

something which is made "to impress the populace" (Rapoport). There are not different "kinds" of architecture, but only different situations which require different solutions in order to satisfy man's physical and psychic needs.

My general aim and approach has therefore been the same in all the writings mentioned above. As time has passed, however, a certain change in method has become manifest. In *Intentions in Architecture* art and architecture were analyzed "scientifically", that is, by means of methods taken over from natural science. I do not think that this approach is wrong, but today I find other methods more illuminating. When we treat architecture analytically, we miss the concrete environmental character, that is, the very quality which is the object of man's identification, and which may give him a sense of existential foothold. To overcome this lack, I introduced in *Existence, Space and Architecture* the concept of "existential space". "Existential space" is not a logico-mathematical term, but comprises the basic relationships between man and his environment. The present book continues the search for a concrete understanding of the environment. The concept of existential space is here divided in the complementary terms "space" and "character", in accordance with the basic psychic functions "orientation" and "identification". Space and character are not treated in a purely philosophical way (as has been done by O. F. Bollnow), but are directly related to architecture, following the definition of architecture as a "concretization of existential space". "Concretization" is furthermore explained by means of the concepts of "gathering" and "thing". The word "thing" originally meant a gathering, and the meaning of anything consists in what it gathers. Thus Heidegger said: "A thing gathers world".

The philosophy of Heidegger has been the catalyst which has made the present book possible and determined its approach. The wish for understanding architecture as a concrete phenomenon, already expressed in *Intentions in Architecture*, could be satisfied in the present book, thanks to Heidegger's essays on language and aesthetics, which have been collected and admirably translated into English by A. Hofstadter (*Poetry, Language, Thought*, New York 1971). First of all I owe to Heidegger the concept of *dwelling*. "Existential foothold" and "dwelling" are synonyms, and "dwelling", in an existential sense, is the purpose of architecture. Man dwells when he can orientate himself within and identify himself with an environment, or, in short, when he experiences the environment as meaningful. Dwelling therefore implies something more than "shelter". It implies that the spaces where life occurs are *places*, in the true sense of the word. A place is a space which has a distinct character. Since ancient times the *genius loci*, or "spirit of place", has been recognized as the concrete reality man has to face and come to terms with in his daily life. Architecture means to visualize the *genius loci*, and the task of the architect is to create meaningful places, whereby he helps man to dwell.

I am well aware of the shortcomings of the present book. Many problems could only be treated in a very sketchy way, and need further elaboration. The book represents, however, a first step towards a "phenomenology of architecture", that is, a theory which understands architecture in concrete, existential terms.

The conquest of the existential dimension is in fact the main purpose of the present book. After decades of abstract, "scientific" theory, it is urgent that we return to a qualitative, phenomenological understanding of architecture. It does not help much to solve practical problems as long as this understanding is lacking. The book therefore does not treat economical and social problems. The existential dimension is not "determined" by the socio-economical conditions, although they may facilitate or impede the (self-) realization of certain existential structures. The socio-economical conditions are like a picture-frame; they offer a certain "space" for life to take place, but do not determine its existential meanings. The existential meanings have deeper roots. They are determined by the structures of our *being-in-the-world*, which have been analyzed by Heidegger in his classical work "Being and Time" (*Sein und Zeit*, 1926). In his essay "Building Dwelling Thinking" (1951), Heidegger moreover related basic existential structures to the functions of building and dwelling, and in "The Thing" (1950) he demonstrated the fundamental importance of the concept of "gathering". Modern architects have in general excluded the existential dimension, although some of them spontaneously recognized its significance. Thus Le Corbusier wrote: "The purpose of architecture is *to move us*. Architectural emotion exists when the work rings within us in tune with a universe whose laws we obey, recognize and respect". (*Vers une architecture*, 1923). Only with Louis Kahn, however, the existential dimension has regained its true importance, and in his question: "What does the building want· to be?", the problem is posed in its essential form.

The existential dimension ("truth") becomes manifest in history, but its meanings transcend the historical situation. History, on the other hand, only becomes meaningful if it represents new concretizations of the existential dimension. In general the concretization of the existential dimension depends on *how*

things are made, that is, it depends on form and technology ("inspired technology", Louis Kahn said). This also includes the "how" of the Natural environment. In the present book we have therefore chosen to approach the existential dimension in terms of place. The place represents architecture's share in truth. The place is the concrete manifestation of man's dwelling, and his identity depends on his belonging to places.

I want to thank all those colleagues and students who have given me inspiration and help. In particular thanks go to my wife Anna Maria De Dominicis for her criticism and untiring help.

Because of the composite nature of the book I have not included any bibliography. All references are found in the foot-notes.

Oslo, June 1976

1. *The Phenomenon of Place*

Our everyday life-world consists of concrete "phenomena". It consists of people, of animals, of flowers, trees and forests, of stone, earth, wood and water, of towns, streets and houses, doors, windows and furniture. And it consists of sun, moon and stars, of drifting clouds, of night and day and changing seasons. But it also comprises more intangible phenomena such as feelings. This is what is "given", this is the "content" of our existence. Thus Rilke asks: "Are we perhaps *here* to say: house, bridge, fountain, gate, jug, fruit tree, window, – at best: column, tower..."[1]. Everything else, such as atoms and molecules, numbers and all kinds of "data", are abstractions or tools which are constructed to serve other purposes than those of everyday life. Today it is common to give more importance to the tools than our life-world.

The concrete things which constitute our given world are interrelated in complex and perhaps contradictory ways. Some of the phenomena may for instance comprise others. The forest consists of trees, and the town is made up of houses. "Landscape" is such a comprehensive phenomenon. In general we may say that some phenomena form an "environment" to others.

A concrete term for environment is *place*. It is common usage to say that acts and occurrences *take place*. In fact it is meaningless to imagine any happening without reference to a locality. Place is evidently an integral part of existence.

What, then, do we mean with the word "place"? Obviously we mean something more than abstract location. We mean a totality made up of concrete things having material substance, shape, texture and colour. Together these things determine an "environmental character",

6

which is the essence of place. In general a place is given as such a character or "atmosphere". A place is therefore a qualitative, "total" phenomenon, which we cannot reduce to any of its properties, such as spatial relationships, without losing its concrete nature out of sight.

Everyday experience moreover tells us that different actions need different environments to take place in a satisfactory way. As a consequence towns and houses consist of a multitude of particular places. This fact is of course taken into consideration by current theory of planning and architecture, but so far the problem has been treated in a too abstract way. "Taking place" is usually understood in a quantitative, "functional" sense, with implications such as spatial distribution and dimensioning. But are not "functions"inter-human and similar everywhere? Evidently not. "Similar" functions, even the most basic ones such as sleeping and eating, take place in very different ways, and demand places with different properties, in accordance with different cultural traditions and different environmental conditions. The functional approach therefore left out the place as a concrete "here" having its particular identity.

Being qualitative totalities of a complex nature, places cannot be described by means of analytic, "scientific" concepts. As a matter of principle science "abstracts" from the given to arrive at neutral, "objective" knowledge. What is lost, however, is the everyday life-world, which ought to be the real concern of man in general and planners and architects in particular[2]. Fortunately a way out of the impasse exists, that is, the method known as *phenomenology*.

Phenomenology was conceived as a "return to things", as opposed to abstractions and mental constructions. So far phenomenologists have been mainly concerned with ontology, psychology, ethics and to some extent aesthetics, and have given relatively little attention to the phenomenology of the daily environment. A few pioneer works however exist, but they hardly contain any direct reference to architecture[3]. A phenomenology of architecture is therefore urgently needed.

Some of the philosophers who have approached the problem of our life-world, have used language and literature as sources of "information". Poetry in fact is able to concretize those totalities which elude science, and may therefore suggest how we might proceed to obtain the needed understanding. One of the poems used by Heidegger to explain the nature of language, is the splendid *A Winter Evening* by Georg Trakl[4]. The words of Trakl also serve our purpose very well, as they make present a total life-situation where the aspect of place is strongly felt.

A WINTER EVENING

Window with falling snow is arrayed,
Long tolls the vesper bell,
The house is provided well,
The table is for many laid.

Wandering ones, more than a few,
Come to the door on darksome courses.
Golden blooms the tree of graces
Drawing up the earth's cool dew.

Wanderer quietly steps within;
Pain has turned the threshold to stone.
There lie, in limpid brightness shown,
Upon the table bread and wine[5].

We shall not repeat Heidegger's profound analysis of the poem, but rather point out a few properties which illuminate our problem. In general, Trakl uses *concrete* images which we all know from our everyday world. He talks about "snow", "window", "house", "table", "door", "tree", "threshold", "bread and wine", "darkness" and "light", and he characterizes man as a "wanderer". These images, however, also imply more general structures. First of all the poem distinguishes between an *outside* and an *inside*. The *outside* is presented in the first two verses of the first stanza, and comprises *natural* as well as *man-made* elements. Natural place is present in the falling snow, which implies winter, and by the evening. The very title of the poem "places" everything in this natural context. A winter evening, however, is something more than a point in the calendar. As a concrete presence, it is experienced as a set of particular qualities, or in general as a *Stimmung* or "character" which forms a background to acts and occurrences. In the poem this character is given by the snow falling on the window, cool, soft and soundless, hiding the contours of those objects which are still recognized in the approaching darkness. The word "falling" moreover creates a sense of *space*, or rather: an implied presence of earth and sky. With a minimum of words Trakl thus brings a total natural environment to life. But the outside also has man-made properties. This is indicated by the vesper bell, which is heard everywhere, and makes the "private" inside become part of a comprehensive, "public" totality. The vesper bell, however, is something more than a practical man-made artifact. It is a symbol, which reminds us of the common values which are at the basis of that totality. In Heidegger's words: "The tolling of the evening bell brings men, as mortals, before the divine"[6].

The *inside* is presented in the next two verses. It is described as a house, which offers man shelter and security by being enclosed and "well provided". It has however a window, an opening which

makes us experience the inside as a complement to the outside. As a final focus within the house we find the table, which "is for many laid". At the table men come together, it is the *centre* which more than anything else constitutes the inside. The character of the inside is hardly told, but anyhow present. It is luminous and warm, in contrast to the cold darkness outside, and its silence is pregnant with potential sound. In general the inside is a comprehensible world of *things*, where the life of "many" may take place.

In the next two stanzas the perspective is deepened. Here the *meaning* of places and things comes forth, and man is presented as a wanderer on "darksome courses". Rather than being placed safely within the house he has created for himself, he comes from the outside, from the "path of life", which also represents man's attempt at "orientating" himself in the given unknown environment.

But nature also has another side: it offers the grace of growth and blossom. In the image of the "golden" tree, earth and sky are unified and become a *world*. Through man's labour this world is brought inside as bread and wine, whereby the inside is "illuminated", that is, becomes meaningful.

Without the "sacred" fruits of sky and earth, the inside would remain "empty". The house and the table receive and gather, and bring the world "close". *To dwell in a house therefore means to inhabit the world.* But this dwelling is not easy; it has to be reached on dark paths, and a threshold separates the outside from the inside. Representing the "rift" between "otherness" and manifest meaning, it embodies suffering and is "turned to stone". In the threshold, thus, the *problem* of dwelling comes to the fore[7].

Trakl's poem illuminates some essential

phenomena of our life-world, and in particular the basic properties of place. First of all it tells us that every situation is local as well as general. The winter evening described is obviously a local, nordic phenomenon, but the implied notions of outside and inside are general, as are the meanings connected with this distinction. The poem hence concretizes basic properties of existence. "Concretize" here means to make the general "visible" as a concrete, local situation. In doing this, the poem moves in the opposite direction of scientific thought. Whereas science departs from the "given", poetry brings us back to the concrete things, uncovering the meanings inherent in the life-world[8].

Furthermore Trakl's poem distinguishes between natural and man-made elements, whereby it suggests a point of departure for an "environmental phenomenology".

Natural elements are evidently the primary components of the given, and places are in fact usually defined in geographical terms. We must repeat however, that "place" means something more than location.

Various attempts at a description of natural places are offered by current literature on "landscape", but again we find that the usual approach is too abstract, being based on "functional" or perhaps "visual" considerations[9]. Again we must turn to philosophy for help. As a first, fundamental distinction Heidegger introduces the concepts of "earth" and "sky", and says: "Earth is the serving bearer, blossoming and fruiting, spreading out in rock and water, rising up into plant and animal...". "The sky is the vaulting path of the sun, the course of the changing moon, the glitter of the stars, the year's seasons, the light and dusk of day, the gloom and glow of night, the clemency and inclemency of the weather, the drifting clouds and

blue depth of the ether..."[10]. Like many fundamental insights, the distinction between earth and sky might seem trivial. Its importance however comes out when we add Heidegger's definition of "dwelling": "The way in which you are and I am, the way in which we humans *are* on the earth, is dwelling...". But "on the earth" already means "under the sky"[11]. He also calls what is *between* earth and sky *the world*, and says that "the world is the house where the mortals dwell"[12]. In other words, when man is capable of dwelling the world becomes an "inside". In general, nature forms an extended comprehensive totality, a "place", which according to local circumstances has a particular identity. This identity, or "spirit", may be described by means of the kind of concrete, "qualitative" terms Heidegger uses to characterize earth and sky, and has to take this fundamental distinction as its point of departure. In this way we might arrive at an existentially relevant understanding of *landscape*, which ought to be preserved as the main designation of natural places. Within the landscape, however, there are subordinate places, as well as natural "things" such as Trakl's "tree". In these things the meaning of the natural environment is "condensed".

The man-made parts of the environment are first of all "settlements" of different scale, from houses and farms to villages and towns, and secondly "paths" which connect these settlements, as well as various elements which transform nature into a "cultural landscape". If the settlements are organically related to their environment, it implies that they serve as *foci* where the environmental character is condensed and "explained". Thus Heidegger says: "The single houses, the villages, the towns are works of building which within and around themselves gather the multifarious in-between. The buildings bring

the earth as the inhabited landscape close to man, and at the same time place the closeness of neighbourly dwelling under the expanse of the sky"[13]. The basic property of man-made places is therefore concentration and enclosure. They are "insides" in a full sense, which means that they "gather" what is known. To fulfill this function they have openings which relate to the outside. (Only an *inside* can in fact have openings). Buildings are furthermore related to their environment by resting on the ground and rising towards the sky. Finally the man-made environments comprise artifacts or "things", which may serve as internal foci, and emphasize the gathering function of the settlement. In Heidegger's words: "The thing things world", where "thinging" is used in the original sense of "gathering", and further: "Only what conjoins itself out of world becomes a thing"[14].

Our introductory remarks give several indications about the *structure* of places. Some of these have already been worked out by phenomenologist philosophers, and offer a good point of departure for a more complete phenomenology.

A first step is taken with the distinction of natural and man-made phenomena, or in concrete terms between "landscape" and "settlement". A second step is represented by the categories of earth-sky (horizontal-vertical) and outside-inside.

These categories have spatial implications, and "space" is hence re-introduced, not primarily as a mathematical concept, but as en existential dimension[15]. A final and particularly important step is taken with the concept of "character". Character is determined by *how* things are, and gives our investigation a basis in the concrete phenomena of our everyday life-world. Only in this way we may fully grasp the *genius loci*; the "spirit of place" which

5. Stimmung. Desert village outside Khartoum.
6. Inside. Old Norwegian cottage, Telemark.

the ancients recognized as that "opposite" man has to come to terms with, to be able to dwell[16].

2. The Structure of Place

Our preliminary discussion of the phenomena of place led to the conclusion that the structure of place ought to be described in terms of "landscape" and "settlement", and analyzed by means of the categories "space" and "character". Whereas "space" denotes the three-dimensional organization of the elements which make up a place, "character" denotes the general "atmosphere" which is the most comprehensive property of any place. Instead of making a distinction between space and character, it is of course possible to employ one comprehensive concept, such as "lived space"[17]. For our purpose, however, it is practical to distinguish between space and character. Similar spatial organizations may possess very different characters according to the concrete treatment of the space-defining elements (the *boundary*). In history the basic spatial forms have been given ever new characterizing interpretations[18]. On the other hand it has to be pointed out that the spatial organization puts certain limits to characterization, and that the two concepts are interdependent.

"Space" is certainly no new term in architectural theory. But space can mean many things. In current literature we may distinguish between two uses: space as three-dimensional geometry, and space as perceptual field[19]. None of these however are satisfactory, being abstractions from the intuitive three-dimensional totality of everyday experience, which we may call "concrete space". Concrete human actions in fact do not take place in an homogeneous isotropic space, but in a space distinguished by qualitative differences, such as "up" and "down". In architec-

7. The path of the wanderer. Sacro Speco, Subiaco.

tural theory several attempts have been made to define space in concrete, qualitative terms. Giedion, thus uses the distinction between "outside" and "inside" as the basis for a grand view of architectural history[20]. Kevin Lynch penetrates deeper into the structure of concrete space, introducing the concepts of "node" ("landmark"), "path", "edge" and "district", to denote those elements which form the basis for men's orientation in space[21]. Paolo Portoghesi finally defines space as a "system of places", implying that the concept of space has its roots in concrete situations, although spaces may be *described* by means of mathematics[22]. The latter view corresponds to Heidegger's statement that "spaces receive their being from locations and not from "space"[23]. The outside-inside relation which is a primary aspect of concrete space, implies that spaces possess a varying degree of *extension* and *enclosure*. Whereas landscapes are distinguished by a varied, but basically continuous extension, settlements are enclosed entities. Settlement and landscape therefore have a *figure-ground* relationship. In general any enclosure becomes manifest as a "figure" in relation to the extended ground of the landscape. A settlement loses its identity if this relationship is corrupted, just as much as the landscape loses its identity as comprehensive extension. In a wider context any enclosure becomes a *centre*, which may function as a "focus" for its surroundings. From the centre space extends with a varying degree of continuity (rhythm) in different directions. Evidently the main directions are horizontal and vertical, that is, the directions of earth and sky. *Centralization*, *direction* and *rhythm* are therefore other important properties of concrete space. Finally it has to be mentioned that natural ele-

ments (such as hills) and settlements may be clustered or grouped with a varying degree of *proximity*.

All the spatial properties mentioned are of a "topological" kind, and correspond to the well-known "principles of organization" of Gestalt theory. The primary existential importance of these principles is confirmed by the researches of Piaget on the child's conception of space[24].

Geometrical modes of organization only develop later in life to serve particular purposes, and may in general be understood as a more "precise" definition of the basic topological structures. The topological enclosure thus becomes a circle, the "free" curve a straight line, and the cluster a grid. In architecture geometry is used to make a general comprehensive system manifest, such as an inferred "cosmic order".

Any enclosure is defined by a boundary. Heidegger says: "A boundary is not that at which something stops but, as the Greeks recognized, the boundary is that, from which something begins its presencing"[25]. The boundaries of a built space are known as *floor*, *wall* and *ceiling*. The boundaries of a landscape are structurally similar, and consist of ground, horizon, and sky. This simple structural similarity is of basic importance for the relationship between natural and man-made places. The enclosing properties of a boundary are determined by its *openings*, as was poetically intuited by Trakl when using the images of window, door and threshold. In general the boundary, and in particular the wall, makes the spatial structure visible as continuous or discontinuous extension, direction and rhythm.

"Character" is at the same time a more general and a more concrete concept than "space". On the one hand it denotes a general comprehensive at-

10. *Wall. S. Gimignano, Toscana.*

mosphere, and on the other the concrete form and substance of the space-defining elements. Any real *presence* is intimately linked with a character[26]. A phenomenology of character has to comprise a survey of manifest characters as well as an investigation of their concrete determinants. We have pointed out that different actions demand places with a different character. A dwelling has to be "protective", an office "practical", a ball-room "festive" and a church "solemn". When we visit a foreign city, we are usually struck by its particular character, which becomes an important part of the experience. Landscapes also possess character, some of which are of a particular "natural" kind. Thus we talk about "barren" and "fertile", "smiling" and "threatening" landscapes. In general we have to emphasize that *all places have character*, and that character is the basic mode in which the world is "given". To some extent the character of a place is a function of time; it changes with the seasons, the course of the day and the weather, factors which above all determine different conditions of *light*.

The character is determined by the material and formal constitution of the place. We must therefore ask: *how* is the ground on which we walk, *how* is the sky above our heads, or in general; *how* are the boundaries which define the place. How a boundary is depends upon its formal articulation, which is again related to the way it is "built". Looking at a building from this point of view, we have to consider how it rests on the ground and how it rises towards the sky.

Particular attention has to be given to its lateral boundaries, or walls, which also contribute decisively to determine the character of the *urban* environment.

We are indebted to Robert Venturi for having recognized this fact, after it had been considered for many years "im-

14

moral" talk about "façades"[27]. Usually the character of a "family" of buildings which constitute a place, is "condensed" in characteristic *motifs*, such as particular types of windows, doors and roofs. Such motifs may become "conventional elements", which serve to transpose a character from one place to another. In the boundary, thus, character and space come together, and we may agree with Venturi when he defines architecture as "the wall between the inside and the outside"[28].

Except for the intuitions of Venturi, the problem of character has hardly been considered in current architectural theory. As a result, theory has to a high extent lost contact with the concrete life-world. This is particularly the case with technology, which is today considered a mere means to satisfy practical demands. Character however, depends upon *how things are made*, and is therefore determined by the technical realization ("building"). Heidegger points out that the Greek word *techne* meant a creative "re-vealing" (*Entbergen*) of truth, and belonged to *poiesis*, that is, "making"[29]. A phenomenology of place therefore has to comprise the basic modes of construction and their relationship to formal articulation. Only in this way architectural theory gets a truly concrete basis.

The structure of place becomes manifest as environmental totalities which comprise the aspects of character and space. Such places are known as "countries", "regions", "landscapes", "settlements" and "buildings". Here we return to the concrete "things" of our everyday life-world, which was our point of departure, and remember Rilke's words: "Are we perhaps *here* to say..." When places are classified we should therefore use terms such as "island", "promontory", "bay", "forest", "grove", or "square", "street", "courtyard", and "floor",

"wall", "roof", "ceiling", "window" and "door".

Places are hence designated by *nouns*. This implies that they are considered real "things that exist", which is the original meaning of the word "substantive". Space, instead, as a system of relations, is denoted by *prepositions*. In our daily life we hardly talk about "space", but about things that are "over" or "under", "before" or "behind" each other, or we use prepositions such as "at", "in", "within", "on", "upon", "to", "from", "along", "next". All these prepositions denote topological relations of the kind mentioned before. Character, finally, is denoted by *adjectives*, as was indicated above. A character is a complex totality, and a single adjective evidently cannot cover more than one aspect of this totality. Often, however, a character is so distinct that one word seems sufficient to grasp its essence. We see, thus, that the very structure of everyday language confirms our analysis of place.

Countries, regions, landscapes, settlements, buildings (and their sub-places) form a series with a gradually diminishing scale. The steps in this series may be called "environmental levels"[30]. At the "top" of the series we find the more comprehensive natural places which "contain" the man-made places on the "lower" levels. The latter have the "gathering" and "focusing" function mentioned above. In other words, man "receives" the environment and makes it focus in buildings and things. The things thereby "explain" the environment and make its character manifest. Thereby the things themselves become meaningful. That is the basic function of *detail* in our surroundings[31]. This does not imply, however, that the different levels must have the same structure. Architectural history in fact shows that this is rarely the case. Vernacular settlements usually

have a topological organization, although the single houses may be strictly geometrical. In larger cities we often find topologically organized neighbourhoods within a general geometrical structure, etc. We shall return to the particular problems of structural correspondence later, but have to say some words about the main "step" in the scale of environmental levels: the relation between natural and man-made places.

Man-made places are related to nature in three basic ways. Firstly, man wants to make the natural structure more precise. That is, he wants to *visualize* his "understanding" of nature, "expressing" the existential foothold he has gained. To achieve this, he *builds* what he has seen. Where nature suggests a delimited space he builds an enclosure; where nature appears "centralized", he erects a *Mal*[32]; where nature indicates a direction, he makes a path. Secondly, man has to *complement* the given situation, by adding what it is "lacking". Finally, he has to *symbolize* his understanding of nature (including himself). Symbolization implies that an experienced meaning is "translated" into another medium. A natural character is for instance translated into a building whose properties somehow make the character manifest[33]. The purpose of symbolization is to free the meaning from the immediate situation, whereby it becomes a "cultural object", which may form part of a more complex situation, or be moved to another place. All the three relationships imply that man *gather* the experienced meanings to create for himself an *imago mundi* or *microcosmos* which concretizes his world. Gathering evidently depends on symbolization, and implies a transposition of meanings to another place, which thereby becomes an existential "centre".

Visualization, complementation and symbolization are aspects of the general processes of settling; and dwelling, in the existential sense of the word, depends on these functions. Heidegger illustrates the problem by means of the *bridge*; a "building" which visualizes, symbolizes and gathers, and makes the environment become a unified whole. Thus he says: "The bridge swings over the stream with case and power. It does not just connect banks that are already there, the banks emerge as banks only as the bridge crosses the stream. The bridge designedly causes them to lie across from each other. One side is set off against the other by the bridge. Nor do the banks stretch along the stream as indifferent border strips of the dry land. With the banks, the bridge brings to the stream the one and the other expanse of the landscape lying behind them. It brings stream and bank and land into each other's neighborhood. The bridge gathers the earth as landscape around the stream"[34]. Heidegger also describes *what* the bridge gathers and thereby uncovers its value as a symbol. We cannot here enter into these details, but want to emphasize that the landscape as such gets its value *through* the bridge. Before, the meaning of the landscape was "hidden", and the building of the bridge brings it out into the open. "The bridge gathers Being into a certain "location" that we may call a "place". This "place", however, did not exist as an entity before the bridge (although there were always many "sites" along the river-bank where it could arise), but comes-to-presence with and as the bridge"[35]. The existential purpose of building (architecture) is therefore to make a site become a place, that is, to uncover the meanings potentially present in the given environment.

The structure of a place is not a fixed, eternal state. As a rule places change, sometimes rapidly. This does not mean, however, that the *genius loci* necessarily changes or gets lost. Later we shall show that *taking place* presupposes that the places conserve their identity during a certain stretch of time. *Stabilitas loci* is a necessary condition for human life. How then is this stability compatible with the dynamics of change? First of all we may point out that any place ought to have the "capacity" of receiving *different* "contents", naturally within certain limits[36]. A place which is only fitted for one particular purpose would soon become useless. Secondly it is evident that a place may be "interpreted" in different ways. To protect and conserve the genius loci in fact means to concretize its essence in ever new historical contexts. We might also say that the history of a place ought to be its "self-realization". What was there as possibilities at the outset, is uncovered through human action, illuminated and "kept" in works of architecture which are simultaneously "old and new"[37]. A place therefore comprises properties having a varying degree of invariance.

In general we may conclude that *place* is the point of departure as well as the goal of our structural investigation; at the outset place is presented as a given, spontaneously experienced totality, at the end it appears as a structured world, illuminated by the analysis of the aspects of space and character.

3. The Spirit of Place

Genius loci is a Roman concept. According to ancient Roman belief every "independent" being has its *genius*, its guardian spirit. This spirit gives life to people and places, accompanies them from birth to death, and determines their character or essence. Even the gods had their *genius*, a fact which illustrates the fundamental nature of the concept[38]. The *genius* thus denotes what a thing *is*, or what it "wants to be", to use a word of Louis Kahn. It is not necessary in our context to go into the history of the concept of *genius* and its relationship to the *daimon* of the Greeks. It suffices to point out that ancient man experienced his environment as consisting of definite characters. In particular he recognized that it is of great existential importance to come to terms with the *genius* of the locality where his life takes place. In the past survival depended on a "good" relationship to the place in a physical as well as a psychic sense. In ancient Egypt, for instance, the country was not only cultivated in accordance with the Nile floods, but the very structure of the landscape served as a model for the lay-out of the "public" buildings which should give man a sense of secutiry by symbolizing an eternal environmental order[39].

During the course of history the *genius loci* has remained a living reality, although it may not have been expressively named as such. Artists and writers have found inspiration in local character and have "explained" the phenomena of everyday life as well as art, referring to landscapes and urban milieus. Thus Goethe says: "It is evident, that the eye is educated by the things it sees from childhood on, and therefore Venetian painters must see everything clearer and with more joy than other people"[40].

Still in 1960 Lawrence Durrell wrote: "As you get to know Europe slowly, tasting the wines, cheeses and characters of the different countries you begin to realize that the important determinant of any culture is after all the spirit of place"[41].

Modern turism proves that the experience of different places is a major human interest, although also this value today tends to get lost. In fact modern man for a long time believed that science and technology had freed him from a direct dependence on places[42].

18

This belief has proved an illusion; pollution and environmental chaos have suddenly appeared as a frightening *nemesis*, and as a result the problem of place has regained its true importance.

We have used the word "dwelling" to indicate the total man-place relationship. To understand more fully what this word implies, it is useful to return to the distinction between "space" and "character". When man dwells, he is simultaneously located in space and exposed to a certain environmental character. The two psychological functions involved, may be called "orientation" and "identification"[43]. To gain en existential foothold man has to be able to *orientate* himself; he has to know *where* he is. But he also has to *identify* himself with the environment, that is, he has to know *how* he is a certain place.

The problem of orientation has been given a considerable attention in recent theoretical literature on planning and architecture. Again we may refer to the work of Kevin Lynch, whose concepts of "node", "path" and "district" denote the basic spatial structures which are the object of man's orientation. The perceived interrelationship of these elements constitute an "environmental image", and Lynch asserts: "A good environmental image gives its possessor an important sense of emotional security"[44]. Accordingly all cultures have developed "systems of orientation", that is, "spatial structures which facilitate the development of a good environmental image". "The world may be organized around a set of focal points, or be broken into named regions, or be linked by remembered routes"[45]. Often these systems of orientation are based on or derived from a given natural structure. Where the system is weak, the image-making becomes difficult, and man feels "lost". "The terror of being lost comes from the necessity that a mobile or-

20. *Identification. Nordic winter.*
21. *Identification. Khartoum, Sudan.*

ganism be oriented in its surroundings"[46]. To be lost is evidently the opposite of the feeling of security which distinguishes dwelling. The environmental quality which protects man against getting lost, Lynch calls "imageability", which means "that shape, color or arrangement which facilitates the making of vividly identified, powerfully structured, highly useful mental images of the environment"[47]. Here Lynch implies that the elements which constitute the spatial structure are concrete "things" with "character" and "meaning". He limits himself, however, to discuss the spatial function of these elements, and thus leaves us with a fragmentary understanding of dwelling. Nevertheless, the work of Lynch constitutes an essential contribution to the theory of place. Its importance also consists in the fact that his empirical studies of concrete urban structure confirm the general "principles of organization" defined by Gestalt psychology and by the researches into child psychology of Piaget[48].

Without reducing the importance of orientation, we have to stress that dwelling above all presupposes *identification* with the environment. Although orientation and identification are aspects of one total relationship, they have a certain independence within the totality. It is evidently possible to orientate oneself without true identification; one gets along without feeling "at home". And it is possible to feel at home without being well acquainted with the spatial structure of the place, that is, the place is only experienced as a gratifying general character. True belonging however presupposes that both psychological functions are fully developed. In primitive societies we find that even the smallest environmental details are known and meaningful, and that they make up complex spatial

20

structures[49]. In modern society, however, attention has almost exclusively been concentrated on the "practical" function of orientation, whereas identification has been left to chance. As a result true dwelling, in a psychological sense, has been substituted by alienation. It is therefore urgently needed to arrive at a fuller understanding of the concepts of "identification" and "character".

In our context "identification" means to become "friends" with a particular environment. Nordic man has to be friend with fog, ice and cold winds; he has to enjoy the creaking sound of snow under the feet when he walks around, he has to experience the poetical value of being immersed in fog, as Hermann Hesse did when he wrote the lines: "Strange to walk in fog! Lonely is every bush and stone, no tree sees the other, everything is alone..."[50]. The Arab, instead, has to be a friend of the infinitely extended, sandy desert and the burning sun. This does not mean that his settlements should not protect him against the natural "forces"; a desert settlement in fact primarily aims at the exclusion of sand and sun and therefore complements the natural situation. But it implies that the environment is experienced as *meaningful*. Bollnow says appropriately: "*Jede Stimmung ist Übereinstimmung*", that is, every character consists in a correspondence between outer and inner world, and between body and psyche"[51]. For modern urban man the friendship with a natural environment is reduced to fragmentary relations. Instead he has to identify with man-made things, such as streets and houses. The German-born American architect Gerhard Kallmann once told a story which illustrates what this means. Visiting at the end of the Second World War his native Berlin after many years of absence, he wanted to see the house where he had grown

up. As must be expected in Berlin, the house had disappeared, and Mr. Kallmann felt somewhat lost. Then he suddenly recognized the typical pavement of the sidewalk: the floor on which he had played as a child. And he experienced a strong feeling of having returned home.

The story teaches us that the objects of identification are concrete environmental properties and that man's relationship to these is usually developed during childhood. The child grows up in green, brown or white spaces; it walks or plays on sand, earth, stone or moss, under a cloudy or serene sky; it grasps and lifts hard and soft things; it hears noises, such as the sound of the wind moving the leaves of a particular kind of tree; and it experiences heat and cold. Thus the child gets acquainted with the environment, and develops perceptual *schemata* which determine all future experiences[52]. The schemata comprise universal structures which are inter-human, as well as locally determined and culturally conditioned structures. Evidently every human being has to possess schemata of orientation as well as identification.

The *identity* of a person is defined in terms of the schemata developed, because they determine the "world" which is accessible. This fact is confirmed by common linguistic usage. When a person wants to tell who he is, it is in fact usual to say: "I am a New Yorker", or "I am a Roman". This means something much more concrete than to say: "I am an architect", or perhaps: "I am an optimist". We understand that human identity is to a high extent a function of places and things. Thus Heidegger says: "Wir sind die Be-Dingten"[53]. It is therefore not only important that our environment has a spatial structure which facilitates orientation, but that it consists of concrete objects of identification.

24. *Sidewalk. Berlin.*
25. *Enclosure. Monteriggioni, Toscana.*

Human identity presupposes the identity of place.

Identification and orientation are primary aspects of man's being-in-the-world. Whereas identification is the basis for man's sense of *belonging*, orientation is the function which enables him to be that *homo viator*, which is part of his nature. It is characteristic for modern man that for a long time he gave the role as a wanderer pride of place. He wanted to be "free" and conquer the world. Today we start to realize that true freedom presupposes belonging, and that "dwelling" means belonging to a concrete place.

The word to "dwell" has several connotations which confirm and illuminate our thesis. Firstly it ought to be mentioned that "dwell" is derived from the Old Norse *dvelja*, which meant to linger or remain. Analogously Heidegger related the German "wohnen" to "bleiben" and "sich aufhalten"[54]. Furthermore he points out that the Gothic *wunian* meant to "be at peace", "to remain in peace". The German word for Peace, *Friede*, means to be free, that is, protected from harm and danger. This protection is achieved by means of an *Umfriedung* or enclosure. "Friede" is also related to *zufrieden* (content), *Freund* (friend) and the Gothic *frijōn* (love). Heidegger uses these linguistic relationships to show that *dwelling means to be at peace in a protected place*. We should also mention that the German word for dwelling, *Wohnung*, derives from *das Gewohnte*, which means what is known or habitual. "Habit" and "habitat" show an analoguous relationship. In other words, man knows what has become accessible to him through dwelling. We here return to the *Übereinstimmung* or correspondence between man and his environment, and arrive at the very root of the problem of "gathering". To gather

22

means that the everyday life-world has become "gewohnt" or "habitual". But gathering is a concrete phenomenon, and thus leads us to the final connotation of "dwelling". Again it is Heidegger who has uncovered a fundamental relationship. Thus he points out that the Old English and High German word for "building", *buan*, meant to dwell, and that it is intimately related to the verb *to be*. "What then does *ich bin* mean? The old word *bauen*, to which the *bin* belongs, answers: *ich bin, du bist,* mean: I dwell, you dwell. The way in which you are and I am, the manner in which we humans *are* on earth, is *buan*, dwelling"[55]. We may conclude that dwelling means to gather the world as a concrete building or "thing", and that the archetypal act of building is the *Umfriedung* or enclosure. Trakl's poetic intuition of the inside-outside relationship thus gets its confirmation, and we understand that our concept of *concretization* denotes the essence of dwelling[56].

Man dwells when he is able to concretize the world in buildings and things. As we have mentioned above, "concretization" is the function of the work of art, as opposed to the "abstraction" of science[57]. Works of art concretize what remains "between" the pure objects of science. Our everyday life-world *consists of* such "intermediary" objects, and we understand that the fundamental function of art is to gather the contradictions and complexities of the life-world. Being an *imago mundi*, the work of art helps man to dwell. Hölderlin was right when he said:
"Full of merit, yet poetically, man dwells on this earth".
This means: man's merits do not count much if he is unable to dwell *poetically*, that is, to dwell in the true sense of the word. Thus Heidegger says: "Poetry does not fly above and surmount the earth in order to escape it and hover over it. Poetry is what first brings man into the earth, making him belong to it, and thus brings him into dwelling"[58]. Only poetry in all its forms (also as the "art of living") makes human existence meaningful, and *meaning* is the fundamental human need.

Architecture belongs to poetry, and its purpose is to help man to dwell. But architecture is a difficult art. To make practical towns and buildings is not enough. Architecture comes into being when a "total environment is made visible", to quote the definition of Susanne Langer[59]. In general, this means to concretize the *genius loci*. We have seen that this is done by means of buildings which gather the properties of the place and bring them close to man. The basic act of architecture is therefore to understand the "vocation" of the place. In this way we protect the earth and become ourselves part of a comprehensive totality. What is here advocated is not some kind of "environmental determinism". We only recognize the fact that man *is* an integral part of the environment, and that it can only lead to human alienation and environmental disruption if he forgets that. To belong to a place means to have an existential foothold, in a concrete everyday sense. When God said to Adam: "You shall be a fugitive and a wanderer on the Earth"[60]; he put man in front of his most basic problem: to cross the threshold and regain the lost place.

1. The Phenomena of Natural Place

To be able to dwell between heaven and earth, man has to "understand" these two elements, as well as their interaction. The word "understand" here does not mean scientific knowledge; it is rather an existential concept which denotes the experience of *meanings*. When the environment is meaningful man feels "at home". The places where we have grown up are such "homes"; we know exactly how it feels to walk on that particular ground, to be under that particular sky, or between those particular trees; we know the warm all-embracing sunshine of the South or the mysterious summer nights of the North. In general we know "realities" which carry our existence. But "understanding" goes beyond such immediate sensations. From the beginning of time man has recognized that nature consists of interrelated elements which express fundamental aspects of being. The landscape where he lives is not a mere flux of phenomena, it has structure and embodies meanings. These structures and meanings have given rise to mythologies (cosmogonies and cosmologies) which have formed the basis of dwelling[1]. A phenomenology of natural place ought to take these mythologies as its point of departure. In doing this, we do not have to re-tell the tales, rather we should ask which concrete categories of understanding they represent.

In general any understanding of the natural environment grows out of a primeval experience of nature as a multitude of living "forces". The world is experienced as a "Thou" rather than an "it"[2]. Man was thus imbedded in nature and dependent upon the natural forces. The growth of man's mental faculties proceeds from the grasping of such diffuse qualities, into more articulate experiences where the parts and the interrelationships within the totality

26. *Monte Bianco.*
27. *Vesuvio.*
28. *Rocks at Petra, Jordan.*

are understood. This process may happen in different ways according to the local environment, and it does not mean that the world loses its concrete, live character. Such a loss implies pure *quantification*, and is thus linked with the modern scientific attitude[3]. We may distinguish between five basic modes of mythical understanding, which have different weight in different cultures.

The first mode of natural understanding takes the forces as its point of departure and relates them to concrete natural elements or "*things*"[4]. Most ancient cosmogonies concentrate on this aspect and explain how "everything" has come into being. Usually creation is understood as a "marriage" of *heaven* and *earth*. Thus Hesiod says: "Earth (Gaia) first of all gave birth to a being equal to herself, who could overspread her completely, the starry heaven (Ouranos)..."[5]. This primeval couple generated the gods end the other mythical creatures, that is, all those "forces" which make up the "multifarious in-between". A similar image is found in Egypt where the world was represented as a "space" between heaven (Nut) and earth (Geb); the only difference being that the sexes of the two elements are here exchanged. The earth is the "serving bearer" from which life emerges, the very foundation of existence (*tellus mater*). The sky, instead, is something "high" and inaccessible. Its shape is described by "the vaulting path of the sun", and its properties in general are experienced as transcendence, order and creative power (rain). The sky primarily has "cosmic" implications, whereas the earth may satisfy man's need for protection and intimacy. At the same time, however, the earth constitutes the extended ground on which his actions take place.

The marriage between heaven and earth forms the point of departure for the

29. *The Roman campagna.*
30. *Place in the shadow under a tree. Petra, Jordan.*

further differentiation of "things". The *mountain*, thus, belongs to the earth, but it rises towards the sky. It is "high", it is close to heaven, it is a meeting place where the two basic elements come together. Mountains were therefore considered "centres" through which the *axis mundi* goes, ...a spot where one can pass from one cosmic zone to another"[6]. In other words, mountains are *places* within the comprehensive landscape, places which make the structure of Being manifest. As such they "gather" various properties. To the general ones already mentioned, we must add the hardness and permanence of *stone* as a material. Rocks and stones have been given primary importance by many cultures because of their imperishableness. In general, however, mountains remain "distant" and somewhat frightening, and do not constitute "insides" where man can dwell. In Medieval painting, thus, rocks and mountains were symbols of "wilderness"; a meaning which was still alive in the landscape painting of Romanticism[7].

But there are other kinds of natural "things" which reveal meanings. In the *tree* heaven and earth are also united, not only in a spatial sense because the tree rises up from the ground, but because it grows and is "alive". Every year the tree re-enacts the very process of creation, and "to a primitive religious mind, the tree *is* the universe, and it is so because it reproduces it and sums it up..."[8]. In general *vegetation* is the manifestation of living reality. But vegetation has also forms which are less friendly or even frightening, The *forest*, thus, is primarily a "wilderness" full of strange and menacing forces. Bachelard writes: "We do not have to be long in the woods to experience the rather anxious impression of "going deeper and deeper" into a limitless world. Soon, if we do not know where we are going,

31. *Wood ad Ariccia, Alban hills.*
32. *Norwegian Forest.*

33. *Grove at Khartoum, Sudan.*
34. *Olive grove. S. Gregorio, Catanzaro.*

we no longer know where we are"[9]. Only when the wood is of limited extension and becomes a *grove*, it remains intelligible and positively meaningful. The Paradise has in fact been imagined as a delimited or enclosed grove or garden.

In the images of Paradise we encounter another basic element of ancient cosmogonies: *water*. The very particular nature of water has always been recognized. In the *Genesis*, God separates the dry land from the water after the creation of heaven and earth, light and darkness, and in other cosmogonies water is *the* primeval substance from which all forms come[10]. The presence of water, thus, gives identity to the land, and the legend of the Deluge presents the "loss of place" as a great flood. Although it is the opposite of place, water belongs intimately to living reality. As a fertilizer it even became a symbol of life, and in the images of Paradise four rivers flow from a spring in the very centre. The history of landscape painting illustrates the importance of water as a life-spending element. The "ideal" landscapes of the fifteenth and the sixteenth centuries usually contain a centrally placed river or lake along which man's settlements are located, and from which the cultivated land extends. Later, water is justly understood and depicted as a local element of primary characterizing importance, and in Romantic landscapes, it reappears as a dynamic chthonic force.

Being the primary natural "things", rocks, vegetation and water make a place meaningful or "sacred", to use the term of Mircea Eliade. He writes: "The most primitive of the "sacred places" we know of constituted a microcosm: a landscape of stones, water and trees"[11]. Moreover he points out that "such places are never *chosen* by man, they

36. *Deyr-el-Bahrȳ, temple of Hasepsowe in the landscape.*

are merely discovered by him; in other words the sacred place in some way or another reveals itself to him"[12]. In the environment the sacred places function as "centres"; they serve as objects of man's orientation and identification, and constitute a spatial structure. In man's understanding of nature we thus recognize the origin of the concept of space as a system of places. Only a system of meaningful places makes a truly human life possible.

The second mode of natural understanding consists in abstracting a systematic *cosmic order* from the flux of occurrences. Such an order is usually based on the course of the sun, as the most invariant and grandiose natural phenomenon, and the cardinal points. In some places it may also be related to the local geographical structure, as in Egypt, where the south-north direction of the Nile constitutes a primary element of man's orientation[13]. An order of this kind implies that the world is understood as a structured "space", where the main directions represent different "qualities" or meanings. In ancient Egypt, thus, the east, the direction of the sun's rising, was the domain of birth and life, whereas the west was the domain of death. "When thou settest on the western horizon, the land is in darkness in the manner of death... (but) when the day breaks, as thou rises on the horizon... they awake and stand upon their feet... they live because thou has arisen for them"[14]. The belief in a cosmic order is usually connected with a concrete image of some kind. In Egypt the world was imagined as "a flat platter with a corrugated rim. The inside bottom of this platter was the flat alluvial plain of Egypt, and the corrugated rim was the rim of mountain countries... This platter floated in water... Above the earth was the inverted pan of the sky, setting the outer limit to the universe". Heaven was imagined to rest on four posts at the corners[15]. In the Nordic countries where the sun loses much of its importance, an abstract "heavenly axis" running north-south was imagined, around which the world turns. This axis ends in the Polar Star, where it is carried by a column, an *Irminsul*[16]. A similar *axis mundi* was imagined by the Romans, whose heavenly *cardo* runs south from the Polar Star, crossing at a right angle the *decumanus*, which represents the course of the sun from the east to the west[17]. In Rome, thus, primary elements of Southern and Nordic cosmologies were unified.

The third mode of natural understanding consists in the definition of the *character* of natural places, relating them to basic human traits.

The abstraction of characters was the achievement of the Greeks, and was evidently made possible by the very structure of the Greek landscape. Topographically Greece consists of numerous distinct but varied sites. Each landscape is a clearly delimited, easily imageable "personality"[18]. Intense sunlight and clear air give the forms an unusual presence. "Because of the ordered variety, clarity and scale in the landscape, the human being is neither engulfed nor adrift in Greece. He can come close to the earth to experience either its comfort or its threat"[19]. The basic property of the Greek environment, therefore, is the individual and intelligible character of places. In some places the surroundings appear to offer protection, in others they menace, and in others again we feel at the centre of a well-defined *cosmos*. In some places there are natural elements of a very particular shape or function, such as horned rocks, caves or wells. In "understanding" these characteristics, the Greeks *personified* them as anthropomorfic *gods*, and every place with pronounced properties became a

37. *Delphi, tholos of Athena.*
38. *Delphi, theatre and temple of Apollo.*
39. *Trees and light. Sacro Speco, Subiaco.*

manifestation of a particular god. Places where the fertile earth feels close were dedicated to the old chthonic deities Demeter and Hera, and places where man's intellect and discipline complement and oppose the chthonic forces were dedicated to Apollo. There are places where the environment is experienced as an ordered whole, such as mountains with an all-round view, dedicated to Zeus, and groves close to water or swampy land dedicated to Artemis. Before any temple was built, open-air altars were erected "in the ideal position from which the whole sacred landscape could be grasped"[20]. We understand thus how Greek architecture took the meaningful place as its points of departure. By relating natural and human characters, the Greeks achieved a "reconciliation" of man and nature which is particularly well concretized at Delphi. Here the old symbols of the earth, the *omphalos* or "navel of the world" and *bothros* or offering cave of the Great Goddess of the earth, were enclosed within Apollo's temple. Thus they were taken over by the "new" god and made part of a total vision of nature and man.

But nature also comprises a fourth category of phenomena which are less palpable. *Light* has of course always been experienced as a basic part of reality, but ancient man concentrated his attention on the sun as a "thing", rather than the more general concept of "light". In Greek civilization, however, light was understood as a symbol of knowledge, artistic as well as intellectual, and was connected with Apollo, who absorbed the old sun-god Helios. In Christianity light became an "element" of prime importance, a symbol of conjunction and unity which was connected with the concept of *love*. God was considered *pater luminis*, and "Divine Light" a manifestation of the

spirit. In Byzantine painting Divine Light was concretized as a golden ground which "surrounds the main figures as with a halo of sanctity"[21], stressing the iconographic foci. A sacred place, thus, was distinguished by the presence of light, and accordingly Dante wrote: "The Divine Light penetrates the universe according to its dignity"[22]. The Renaissance, instead, understood the world as a *microtheos* which God is manifest in every thing. As a result, the landscape painters depicted the environment as a totality of "facts", where everything down to the smallest detail seems fully understood and loved. "Facts become art through love, which unifies them and lifts them to a higher plan of reality; and, in landscape, this all embracing love is expressed by light"[23].

Light is not only the most general natural phenomenon, but also the less constant. Light conditions change from morning to evening, and during the night darkness fills the world, as light does during the day. Light, thus, is intimately connected with the *temporal rhythms* of nature which form a fifth dimension of understanding. The phenomena which distinguish a natural place cannot be separated from these rhythms[24]. The seasons, thus, change the appearance of places; in some regions more, in others less. In the northern countries green summers and white winters alternate, and both seasons are characterized by very different conditions of light. The temporal rhythms obviously do not change the basic elements which constitute a natural place, but in many cases they contribute decisively to its character and are therefore often reflected in local myths and fairytales. In landscape painting, the local importance of temporal rhythms and light conditions were studied from the eighteenth century on, a development which culminated with

impressionism[25].

In mythopoeic thought time is just as qualitative and concrete as other natural phenomena, and is experienced in the periodicity and rhythm of man's own life as well as in the life of nature. Man's participation in the natural totality is concretized in *rituals*, in which "cosmic events", such as creation, death and resurrection are re-enacted. As such, rituals do not however belong to the natural environment, and will be discussed in the next chapter, together with the general problem of representing time.

Thing, order, character, light and time are the basic categories of concrete natural understanding. Whereas thing and order, are spatial (in a concrete qualitative sense), character and light refer to the general atmosphere of a place[26]. We may also point out that "thing" and "character" (in the sense here used) are dimensions of the earth, whereas "order" and "light" are determined by the sky. Time, finally, is the dimension of constancy and change, and makes space and character parts of a living reality, which at any moment is given as a particular place, as a *genius loci*. In general the categories designate the *meanings* man has abstracted from the flux of phenomena ("forces"). In his classical work on the relationship between nature and the "human soul", Willy Hellpach calls such meanings "existential contents", and says: "Existential contents have their source in the landscape"[27].

2. *The Structure of Natural place*

The term "natural place" denotes a series of environmental levels, from continents and countries down to the shaded area under an individual tree. All these "places" are determined by the concrete properties of earth and sky. The ground is obviously the most stable

element, although some of its properties change with the seasons, but the more variable and less concrete sky also plays a "characterizing" role of decisive importance. It is natural to take the more stable properties as the point of departure for our discussion, in relation to the environmental level which serves as the comprehensive stage for everyday life, that is: *landscape*.

The distinctive quality of any landscape is *extension*, and its particular character and spatial properties are determined by *how* it extends. Extension, thus, may be more or less continuous, sub-places within the all-embracing landscape may be formed and its capacity of receiving man-made elements varies accordingly. The "how" of extension primarily depends on the nature of the ground, that is, on the topographical conditions. "Topography" simply means "place-description", but it is generally used to denote the physical configuration of a place. In our context "topography" primarily means what geographers call the *surface relief*. On a flat plain, extension is general and infinite, but usually variations in the surface relief create directions and defined spaces.

It is important to distinguish between the structure and the scale of the relief. The structure may be described in terms of nodes, paths and domains, that is, elements which "centralize" space such as isolated hills and mountains or circumscribed basins, elements which direct space such as valleys, rivers and *wadis*, and elements which define an extended spatial pattern, such as a relatively uniform cluster of fields or hills. Evidently the effect of such elements is very different according to their dimensions. For our purpose it is practical to distinguish between three levels: micro, medium and macro. The micro elements define spaces which are too small to serve human purposes, while

42. *Extended land. Valle d'Idria, Puglia.*
43. *Extended land. Romagna.*
44. *Extended land. Norway from the air in winter.*

the macro elements are analogously too large. Spaces which are directly suited for or dimensionally related to human dwelling have a medium or "human" scale. As examples of different environmental scales we may mention the Norvegian forest, the plains of Northern France (the *campagne*), and the rolling countryside of Denmark. In the Norvegian forest the ground is covered by minuscule hillocks and tufts. The ground is never open and free, but cut through by tiny "valleys" between minuscule "hills". A kind of micro-landscape is formed, which seems to have been made for gnomes or dwarfs. In Northern France, instead, the surface relief consistes of extended but low, ondulating mounds, whose super-human scale creates a feeling of infinite, "cosmic", extension. In Denmark the landscape is somewhat similar, but the scale is smaller, and an intimate "human" environment results. If we maintain the "Danish" scale horizontally, but accentuate the vertical dimensions of the relief, a "human hill landscape" is formed. As examples we may mention the central parts of Tuscany and the Monferrato in Italy. Where the depressions reach a certain depth, however, the hills become separated and the ground loses its continuity. As a result the landscape appears forbidding and "wild". This is the case in Liguria, where the land is cut through by a network of narrow ravines[28]. A relatively small change thus suffices to transform the inviting and ordered hill landscape of the neighbour regions into a kind of confused maze.

Our examples have indicated how variations in the surface relief determine the spatial properties of the landscape, and to some extent its character. Characters such as "wild" and "friendly" are thus functions of the relief, although they may be accentuated or contradicted by

45. *Norwegian forest.*
46. *Campagna in Central Italy.*
47. *Rolling countryside in Denmark.*

texture, colour and *vegetation*. The words "texture" and "colour" refer to the material substance of the ground, that is, whether it consists of sand, earth, stone, grass or water, whereas "vegetation" denotes elements which are added to end transform the surface relief. The character of the landscape is evidently to a high extent determined by these "secondary" elements. Similar reliefs may appear as a "barren" desert of "fertile" plain, according to the absence or presence of vegetation. At the same time, however, similar reliefs preserve fundamental common properties, such as "infinite" extension. The undulating plains of Northern France, for instance, possess the "cosmic" quality which is usually found in the desert, but simultaneously the land is fertile. A fascinating synthesis is thus experienced[29].

When vegetation becomes a primary feature, the landscape in general gets its name from this property, as in the various types of forest landscapes. In the forest landscape the surface relief is less prominent than the spatial effect of the vegetation. Often relief and vegetation combine to form very particular landscapes. In Finland, for instance, the continuous forest is "interpenetrated" by a complex system of interconnected lakes. As a result an eminently Nordic character is created, where the microstructure of the forest is emphasized by the mobile and "live" element of the water[30]. In general the presence of *water* adds a certain micro-scale to landscapes whose relief lacks this dimension, or it adds to the mystery of landscapes which already possess the micro level. When water is present as a swift river or cascade, nature itself becomes mobile and dynamic. The reflecting surface of lakes and ponds also has a dematerializing effect which counteracts the stable topographical structure. In a swamp landscape, finally, the ground

48. *Hills in the Monferrato.*
49. *Finnish landscape.*
50. *Ravine. Vitorchiano, Lazio.*

51. *Coastline in Basilicata, Maratea.*

52. *Valley in Norway.*
53. *Norwegian islands.*
54. *Norwegian fjord.*

gets a maximum of indeterminacy. The banks of rivers and lakes, on the contrary, form precise edges which usually function as primary structural elements in the landscape. Such edges have the double function of giving definition to the water itself as well as the adjoining land. Evidently this definition may happen on all environmental levels, and on the most comprehensive it is the ocean which forms the "final" ground on which the continents appear as distinct "figures"[31].

Through the interaction of surface, relief, vegetation and water, characteristic totalities or *places* are formed which constitute the basic elements of landscapes. A phenomenology of natural place obviously ought to contain a systematic survey of such concrete totalities[32]. Variations in the surface relief generate a series of places, for which our language has well-known names: plain, valley, basin, ravine, plateau, hill, mountain. All these places possess distinctive phenomenological characteristics. The plain, thus, makes extension as such manifest, whereas the valley is a delimited and directed space. A basin is a centralized valley, where space becomes enclosed and static. Whereas valleys and basins have a macro or medium scale, a ravine (cleft, gorge) is distinguished by a "forbidding" narrowness. It has the quality of an "under-world" which gives access to the "inside" of the earth. In a ravine we feel caught or trapped, and the etymology of the word in fact leads us back to *rapere*, that is to "seize". Hills and mountains are spatial complements to valleys and basins, and function as primary space-defining "things" in the environment. The general structural properties of hills and mountains are denoted by words such as "slope", "crest", "ridge" and "peak". We have already suggested that the presence of water may emphasize the

55. *Clouds. Lüneburger Heide.*
56. *Valley and silhouette. Subiaco.*
57. *From the Syrian desert.*
58. *Countryside in Denmark.*

place-structure of the surface relief. A valley is literally "underlined" by a river, and the image of a basin is strengthened by a lake. But water also generates particular kinds of spatial configurations: island, point, promontory, peninsula, bay and fjord, all of which must be counted among the most distinctive natural places. The island thus, is a place *par excellence*, appearing as an "isolated", clearly defined figure. Existentially the island brings us back to the origins; it rises out of the element from which everything was originally born. The word "peninsula" means "almost an island", and thus language expresses an important spatial structure. A gulf or bay is also a strong archetypal place, which may be characterized as an "inverted peninsula". The typical places generated by vegetation, such as forest, grove, and field, have already been mentioned; we only have to remind of their importance as parts of "living" reality[33].

Being on the earth implies to be under the sky. Although the sky is distant and intangible, it has concrete "properties", and a very important characterizing function. In daily life we take the sky for granted; we notice that it changes with the weather, but hardly recognize its importance for the general "atmosphere". It is only when we visit places very different from our home that we suddenly experience the sky as "low" or "high", or otherwise different from what we are used to. The effect of the sky is basically due to two factors. Firstly the constitution of the sky itself, that is, the quality of light and colour, and the presence of characteristic clouds[34]. Secondly its relationship to the ground, that is, how it appears, from below. Seen from an extended open plain, the sky becomes a complete hemisphere, and when the weather is "good", its appearance is all-embracing and truly grandiose. In places with a pronounced surface relief or rich vegetation, however, only a sector of the sky is seen at the time. Space contracts, and the landscape becomes intimate or even constricted. That this is not a modern experience, is confirmed by the report of an ancient Egyptian scribe: "Thou hast not trodden the road to Meger (in Syria), in which the sky is dark by day, which is overgrown with cypresses, oaks and cedars that reach the heavens... Shuddering seizes thee, (the hair of) thy head stands on end and the soul lies in thy hand... The ravine is on one side of thee, while the mountain rises on the other"[35]. A frightening experience indeed for an Egyptian who was used to see the sun in all its course. In general we may say that *the sky is as large as the space from which it is seen*. Remembering that a space begins its "presencing" from the boundary, we understand how the *silhouette* of the surrounding "walls" becomes important when the space is narrow. Instead of being a comprehensive hemisphere within a linear *horizon*, the sky is reduced to a background for the contours of the surface relief. The landscape character thus becomes manifest as a silhouette against the sky, sometimes gently undulating, sometimes serrate and wild[36].

The climatically determined appearance of the sky acts as a counterpoint to its general spatial properties. In the desert areas of North Africa and the Near East, the cloudless blue sky gives emphasis to the infinite extension of the land, and we experience the landscape as embodying an eternal order, centered on ourselves. On the plains of Northern Europe, instead, the sky is usually "low" and "flat". Even on cloudless days its colour is relatively pale, and the feeling of being under an embracing dome is usually absent. The horizontal direction is therefore experienced as mere ex-

tension. Many variations are however possible according to the local surface relief and the quality of the light. In areas which are not too distant from the coast, the atmospheric conditions are continuously changing and light becomes a live and strongly poetic element. In a country like Holland, where the ground is flat and subdivided in small spaces, light remains a local and intimate value. In Northern France, instead, the landscape opens up and the extended sky becomes a comprehensive "stage" for the continuously changing quality of light. A "light-world" is experienced, which evidently inspired the luminous walls of the Gothic cathedrals and the impressionistic paintings of Monet[37]. In Southern Europe these poetic qualities of light are mostly absent; the strong and warm sun "fills the space" and brings out the plastic qualities of natural forms and "things". As a consequence, Italian landscape painting has always concentrated its attention on the sculptural object, and depicts an environment consisting of evenly illuminated discrete objects[38].

In general the earth is the "stage" where man's daily life takes place. To some extent it may be controlled end shaped, and a friendly relationship results. Natural landscape thus becomes *cultural landscape*, that is, an environment where man has found his meaningful place within the totality. The sky, instead, remains distant and is distinguished by its "otherness". In structural terms these basic facts are expressed by the *horizontal* and the *vertical*. The simplest model of man's existential space is therefore a horizontal plane pierced by a vertical axis[39]. On the plane man choses and creates centres, paths and domains which make up the concrete space of his everyday world.

Our brief excursion into the structure of natural place has implied that it pos-

sesses on several "levels". A whole country may be the object of concrete identification, in accordance with its particular structure. Italy is thus distinguished by its being a peninsula with a chain of mountains in the middle. On both sides of the central ridge, landscapes of various kinds are formed: plains, valleys, basins and bays, which, because of the topography of the country, maintain a certain independence. Within the landscapes, sub-places offer man the possibility of intimate dwelling. Among the sub-places we also find the archetypal *retreat* where man may still experience the presence of the original forces of the earth. The "Carceri" of St. Francis outside Assisi or the Sacro Speco of St. Benedict near Subiaco are characteristic examples. In these places the saints of the Middle Ages experienced the mystery of nature, which to them meant the presence of God[40]. Being a peninsula divided by a range of mountains, Scandinavia is structurally similar to Italy. But the dimensions are larger, and the spatial properties of the regions more varied. As a result, the peninsula comprises *two* countries with distinct characteristics, whereas it would not make sense to split Italy longitudinally in "halves". In southern Norway we find a primary "hand-shaped" system of valleys with the centre in Oslo, which therefore acts as a natural focus. Western Norway is subdivided by a series of parallel fjords between tall mountains, and therefore consists of more separate, albeit "similar" landscapes. Northern Sweden possesses an analogous system of long, parallel valleys, whereas the southern part of the country rather may be called a cluster of domains defined by lakes and hills. The coast of both countries is accompanied by a belt of islands and skerries, which introduces a "microstructure" entirely lacking in Italy.

59. *Scandinavia, map.*
60. *Assisi, Eremo delle Carceri.*

61. *Italy, map.*

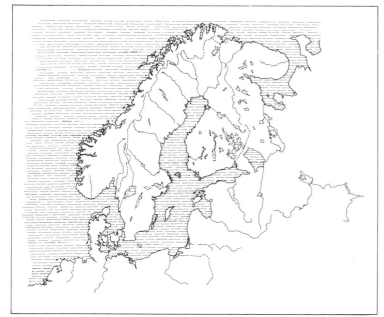

Structurally orientation and identification thus means the experience of natural place within natural place. The different "insides" are "known" in accordance with their structural properties. In all countries in fact we find that the naming of regions and landscapes reflect the existence of natural places which have a structurally determined identity[41]. The individual *genius loci* is therefore part of a hierarchical system, and must be seen in this context to be fully understood.

3. The spirit of Natural Place

Our discussion of the phenomena of natural place has uncovered several basic types of natural factors, which in general are related to the earth or the sky, or express an interaction of the two basic "elements". Our discussion has furthermore implied that in some regions the sky may appear the dominant factor, whereas in others the earth contributes the primary presence. Although some kind of interaction between the two elements exists everywhere, there are places where sky and earth seem to have realized a particularly happy "marriage". In these places the environment becomes manifest as a harmonious whole of medium scale which allows for relatively easy and complete identification. Among the landscapes where the sky dominates we may distinguish between those where the "cosmic order" is of primary importance and those where the changing atmospheric conditions contribute decisively to the environmental character. Where the earth is dominant, a classification must be based on the presence of archetypal "things" as well as variations in scale (micro-macro).

Romantic Landscape

It is natural to start a discussion of archetypal natural places with the kind of landscape where the original forces are still most strongly felt: the Nordic forest, as it is known in certain parts of Central Europe and particularly in Scandinavia. The Nordic forest is distinguished by an interminable multitude of different phenomena:

The ground is rarely continuous, but it is subdivided and has a varied relief; rocks and depressions, groves and glades, bushes and tufts create a rich "microstructure".

The sky is hardly experienced as a total hemisphere, but is narrowed in between the contours of trees and rocks, and is moreover continuously modified by clouds.

The sun is relatively low and creates a varied play of spots of light and shadow, with clouds and vegetation acting as enriching "filters". Water is ever present as a dynamic element, both as running streams and quiet, reflecting ponds.

The quality of the air is constantly changing, from moist fog to refereshing ozone.

As a whole, the environment seems to make a mutable and rather incomprehensible world manifest, where surprises belong to the order of the day. The general instability is emphasized by the contrast between the seasons and by frequent changes of weather. In general we may say that the Nordic landscape is characterized by *an indefinite multitude of different places*. Behind every hillock and rock there is a new place, and only exceptionally the landscape is unified to form a simple, univocal space. In the Nordic landscape therefore, men encounters a host of natural "forces", whereas a general unifying order is lacking. This becomes clearly manifest in the literature, art and music of the Nordic countries, where natural impressions and moods play a primary role. In legends and fairy-tales we encounter the mythical inhabitants of this world: gnomes, dwarfs and trolls[42]. Still today Nordic man carries these beings within his psyche, and when he wants to "live", he leaves the city to experience the mysteries of the Nordic landscape. In doing this he looks for the *genius loci*, which he has to understand to gain an existential foothold. In general we may characterize the Nordic world as a *romantic* world, in the sense that it brings man back to a distant "past", which is experienced emotionally rather than understood as allegory or history.

What kind of dwelling is possible in the Nordic landscape? We have already suggested that Nordic man has to approach nature with *empathy*, he has to live *with* nature in an intimate sense. Direct participation is thus more important than abstraction of elements and order. This participation, however, is not social. Rather it implies that the individual finds his own "hiding-place" in nature. "My home is my castle", is in fact a Nordic saying. The process of empathy and participation obviously takes place in different ways in different regions. In Denmark, where the scale is human and idyllic, dwelling means to settle between the low mounds, under the large trees, embraced by the changing sky. In Norway, instead, it means to find a place in "wild" nature, between rocks and dark, gloomy conifers, preferably next to a swift stream of water[43]. In both cases however, the "forces" of nature are present and make dwelling become am *interaction* between man and his environment. The essential property which makes these forces manifest, is microstructure. The Nordic landscape is therefore dominated by the *earth*. It is a chthonic landscape, which does not with ease rise up to approach the sky, and its character is determined by an

62. *Living between and under the trees. Denmark.*
63. *Romantic landscape. Norwegian forest.*
64. *Microstructure. Norwegian forest.*

interacting multitude of unintelligible detail.

Cosmic Landscape

In the *desert* the complexities of our concrete life-world are reduced to a few, simple phenomena[44]:

The infinite extension of the monotonous barren ground; the immense, embracing vault of the cloudless sky (which is rarely experienced as a sector between rocks and trees); the burning sun which gives an almost shadowless light; the dry, warm air, which tells us how important breathing is for the experience of place.

As a whole, the environment seems to make an absolute and eternal order manifest, a world which is distinguished by permanence and structure. Even the dimension of time does not introduce any ambiguities. The course of the sun thus describes an almost exact meridian, and divides space into "orient", "occident", "midnight", and "midday", that is, *qualitative* domains which in the South are commonly used as denotations for the cardinal points[45]. Sunset and sunrise connect day and night without transitional effects of light, and create a simple temporal rhythm. Even the animals of the desert participate in the infinite, monotonous environmental rhythms, as it becomes manifest in the movements of the camel, "the ship of the desert".

The only surprise one might encounter in the desert is the sand-storm, the *haboob* of the Arabs. But the sandstorm is also monotonous. It does not represent a different kind of order; it hides the world, but does not change it.

In the desert, thus, the *earth* does not offer man a sufficient existential foothold. *It does not contain individual places*, but forms a continuous neutral ground. The *sky*, instead, is structured by the sun (and also by the moon and the stars) and its simple order is not obscured by atmospheric changes. In the desert, therefore, man does not encounter the multifarious "forces" of nature, but experiences its most absolute cosmic properties. This is the existential situation behind the Arabic proverb: "The further you go into the desert, the closer you come to God". The belief that there is only one God, monotheism, has in fact come into being in the desert countries of the Near East. Both Judaism and Christianity stem from the desert, although their doctrines have become "humanized" by the more friendly landscape of Palestine. In Islam, however, the desert has found its supreme expression. For the Muslim the conception of the one God is the only dogma, and five times a day he turns towards Mecca to say: "*la ilaha ill-allah*", there is no God but Allah"[46]. By thus proclaiming the unity of God, the Muslim confirms the unity of his world, a world which has the *genius loci* of the desert as its natural model. For the desert-dweller the *genius loci* is a manifestation of the Absolute[47]. Existentially, the desert *is* in a very particular way, and its being has to be known as such to make dwelling possible. Islam therefore confirms that the Arab has become a friend of the desert. It is no longer understood as "death", as it was by the ancient Egyptians, but has become a basis for life. This does not mean however, that the Arab *settles* in the desert. For settling he needs the *oasis*, that is, he needs an intimate place within the cosmic macroworld[48]. In the oasis the slender trunks of the palms which rise from the flat expanse of the ground seem to make the order of horizontals and verticals which constitute Arabic space manifest. Within this abstract order no truly plastic objects are possible, the "play of light and shadow" is extinguished, and everything is reduced to surface and line. In the oasis dwelling gets its full range, comprising the totality as well as the individual locality.

Classical Landscape

Between the South and the North we find the classical landscape. It was "discovered" in Greece, and later it became one of the primary components of the Roman environment. The classical landscape is neither characterized by monotony nor by multifariousness. Rather we find an intelligible *composition* of distinct elements: clearly defined hills and mountains which are rarely covered by the shaggy woods of the North, clearly delimited, imageable natural spaces such as valleys and basins, which appear as individual "worlds"; a strong and evenly distributed light and a transparent air which give the forms a maximum of sculptural presence. The ground is simultaneously continuous and varied, and the sky is high and embracing without however possessing the absolute quality encountered in the desert. A true microstructure is lacking, all dimensions are "human" and constitute a total, harmonious equilibrium. The environment thus consists of palpable "things" which stand out (ek-sist) in light. The classic landscape "receives" light without losing its concrete presence[49].

In general the classical landscape may be described as a *meaningful order of distinct, individual places*. Thus Ludwig Curtius writes: "The single Greek landscape is naturally given as a dearly delimited unit, which to the eye appears as an integrated totality (*geschlossenes Gebilde*). The Greek sense for plastic form and boundary, for the whole and the parts, is founded on the landscape..."[50].We have already pointed out that the Greeks personified the various characters experienced in the landscape

as anthropomorphic *gods*, interrelating thus natural and human properties. In nature Greek man found himself, rather than the absolute God of the desert or the trolls of the Nordic forest. That means that by knowing himself he knew the world, and became freed from the total abstraction as well as the empathy discussed in connection with the cosmic and the romantic landscapes. The classical landscape therefore makes a human fellowship possible, where every part conserves its identity within the totality. Here the individual neither is absorbed by an abstract system, nor has to find his private hiding-place. A true "gathering" thus becomes possible, which fulfills the most basic aspects of dwelling.

How then does "classical man" dwell in the landscape? Basically we may say that he places himself in front of nature as an equal "partner". He is where he is, and looks at nature as a friendly complement to his own being. This simple and stable relationship helps to release human *vitality*, whereas the mutable Nordic world makes man search security in introvert heaviness. When man places himself "in front of" nature, he reduces landscape to a *veduta*, and the classical landscape is in fact hardly "used" in the Nordic sense of "going into nature"[51]. The union of man and nature is rather expressed through the practical use of agriculture, which accentuates the landscape structure as an "addition" of relatively independent, individual places. The *genius loci* of the classical landscape is therefore first of all manifest where clearly defined natural places are emphasized by the loving care of man. As a well known example we may mention the Valdarno in Italy, where the cultural landscape indeed expresses the classical "reconciliation". In general the reconciliation is manifest as a harmonious equilibrium of earth

and sky. Plastically present, the earth rises up without drama, and blossoms in trees which have their individual plastic value. The golden light of the sky answers gently, and promises man "bread and wine".

Complex Landscapes

The romantic, cosmic and classical landscapes are archetypes of natural place. Being generated by the basic relationships between earth and sky, they are relevant categories which may help us to "understand" the genius loci of any concrete situation. As types, however, they hardly appear in "pure" form, but participate in various kinds of syntheses. We have already mentioned the "fertile desert" of the French *campagne*, where cosmic, romantic and classical properties unify to form a particularly meaningful totality, a landscape which made Gothic architecture possible, and hence a particularly complete interpretation of the Christian message. We might also mention a place like Naples, where classical spaces and characters meet the romantic atmosphere of the sea and the chthonic forces of the volcano, or Venice where cosmic extension comes together with the everchanging, glittering surface of the lagoon. In Brandenburg, instead, extension is squeezed in between a sandy moor and a low, grey sky, creating a landscape which seems saturated by the monotonous, cheerless rhythm of marching soldiers. In the Alps, on the contrary, we find a "wild-romantic" character, which is primarily determined by the contrast between serrate silhouettes and impenetrable ravines. The possibilities are legion and determine a corresponding multitude of "existential meanings".

The notion that the landscape determines fundamental existential meanings or contents, is confirmed by the fact

71. *Naples, panorama.*
72. *The crater of the Vesuvio.*
73. *Venice across the lagoon.*
74. *Norwegian landscape.*
75. *Alpine landscape.*

that most people feel "lost" when they are moved to a "foreign" landscape. It is well known that people of the great plains easily suffer from claustrophobia when they have to live in a hilly country, and that those who are used to be surrounded by intimate spaces easily become victims of agoraphobia. In any case, however, landscape functions as an extended *ground* to the man-made places. It contains these places, and as a "preparation" for them, it also contains natural "insides". We have described these as "meaningful places" which are "known" because they possess particular structural properties. Dwelling in nature is therefore not a simple question of "refuge". Rather it means to understand the given environment as a set of "insides", from the macro down to the micro level. In the romantic landscape dwelling means to rise up from the micro to the macro level; here the immediately given are the forces of the earth, whereas God is hidden. In the cosmic landscape the process has the opposite direction, and the enclosed garden or "paradise" becomes the ultimate goal. In the classical landscape, finally, man finds himself in the harmonious "middle" and may reach "out" as well as "in". Rilke told us what it is all about: "Earth, is not this what you want: invisibly to arise in us?"[52].

76. *Urnes Stave church, Norway.*
77. *Megalithic structure. Segni, Lazio.*

1. The Phenomena of Man-made Place

To dwell between heaven and earth means to "settle" in the "multifarious in-between", that is, to concretize the general situation as a man-made place. The word "settle" here does not mean a mere economical relationship; it is rather an existential concept which denotes the ability to symbolize *meanings*. When the man-made environment is meaningful, man is "at home". The places where we have grown up are such "homes"; we know exactly how it feels to walk on that particular pavement, to be between those particular walls, or under that particular ceiling; we know the cool. enclosure of the Southern house, and the conforting warmth of the Nordic dwelling. In general, we know "realities" which carry our existence. But "settling" goes beyond such immediate gratifications. From the beginning of time man has recognized that to create a place means to express the essence of being. The man-made environment where he lives is not a mere practical tool or the result of arbitrary happenings, it has structure and embodies meanings. These meanings and structures are reflections of man's understanding of the natural environment and his existential situation in general[1]. A study of man-made place therefore ought to have a *natural* basis: it should take the relationship to the natural environment as its point of departure. Architectural history shows that man's primeval experience of everything as a "Thou", also determined his relationship to buildings and artifacts. Like natural elements, they were imbued with life, they had *mana*, or magical power. Demonic powers in fact are conquered by giving them a "dwelling". In this way they are fixed to a place and may be influenced by man[2]. The architecture of early civilizations may therefore be interpreted as a concretization of the under-

standing of nature, described above in terms of things, order, character, light and time. The processes involved in "translating" these meanings into man-made forms have already been defined as "visualization", "complementation", and "symbolization", whereas "gathering" serves the somewhat different purpose of making the man-made place become a *microcosmos*. In general we may say that man "builds" his world.

The first mode of building consists in concretizing the natural forces. In the early history of Western art and architecture we encounter two basic ways of doing this. Either the forces are "directly" expressed by means of lines and ornament, or they are concretized as man-made things, which represent the natural things mentioned above. Whereas the first way was employed by the "Nordic" peoples, the second was developed by the Mediterranean civilizations[3]. We shall here concentrate our attention on the "Mediterranean" mode. Early Mediterranean architecture is first of all distinguished by the use of large *stones*. It is a *megalithic* architecture where the material symbolizes the solidity and permanence found in mountains and rocks. Permanence was understood as a primary existential need, and was related to man's ability of procreation. The erect stone, *menhir*, was simultaneously a "built" rock and a phallic symbol, and the massive, cyclopic wall embodied the same forces[4]. Through a process of abstraction, the elementary forces were transformed into a system of verticals and horizontals ("active" and "passive" elements), a development which culminated in the orthogonal structures of Egyptian architecture. Other natural meanings were also related to this system. The Egyptian pyramids are "artificial mountains" which were built to make the properties of a real mountain manifest, such as an

inferred vertical axis which connects earth and sky and "receives" the sun. Thus the pyramid unifies the primordial mountain of Egyptian mythology with the radiant sun-god Ra, and represents the king as his son. At the same time the pyramids through their location between oasis and desert (life and death), visualize the spatial structure of the country; a longitudinal fertile valley between infinite expanses of barren land[5]. Here buildings are used to define a significant boundary ("edge"). Finally we may mention that Egyptians "built" the sky, decorating ceilings of tombs, temples and houses with stars on a blue ground. By means of visualization and symbolization the ancient Egyptians thus concretized their known world.

We gave already mentioned the *cave* as another archetypal natural element. In megalithic architecture artificial caves, *dolmen*, were built to visualize this aspect of the earth. Being simultaneously interior spaces and feminine symbols, the artificial caves were understood as representations of the world as a whole[6], an interpretation which was completed by the introduction of vertical "masculine" elements, such as a pillar, or an orthogonal system of vertical and horizontal members. The "marriage of heaven and earth" which was the point of departure for ancient cosmogonies was thus concretized in built form. Typical examples are furnished by the megalithic temples of Malta, where the apses contained a *menhir* and the boundaries are orthogonally articulated.

In ancient architecture we also encounter other representations of natural elements. The Ionic temple with its numerous columns has thus been described as a "sacred grove", and the expression "forest of columns" is often used to designate the hypostyle halls of early civilizations. In the Egyptian temples the columns are in fact derived from plant forms, such as palm, papyrus and lotus. The Egyptian forest of columns represented "the land and the sacred plants which rose out of the fertilized soil to bring protection, permanence and sustenance to the land and its people"[7]. In general man's understanding of the fertile soil is visualized through *agriculture*. In the cultural landscape the natural forces are "domesticated" and living reality is made manifest as an ordered process where man participates. The *garden* is hence a place where living nature is concretized as an organic totality. Man's image of Paradise was in fact always an enclosed garden. In the garden the known elements of nature are gathered: fruit trees, flowers and "tamed" water. In Mediaeval painting it is depicted as a *hortus conclusus* with the "Tree of Life" and a fountain in the middle, surrounded by a "wilderness" of mountains and forests[8]. Even water may thus be "built", that is, given precise definition as part of a cultural landscape, or visualized in a fountain. In the cultural landscape man "builds" the earth, and makes its potential structure manifest as a meaningful totality. A cultural landscape is based on "cultivation", and contains defined places, paths and domains which concretize man's understanding of the natural environment.

Orthogonal space, cave-like interior and cultural landscape suggest general comprehensive orders, which to some extent satisfy man's need for understanding nature as a structured whole, comprising all environmental levels from the artifact to the region. The quest for order, however, above all becomes manifest through the "building" of one of the *cosmic orders* mentioned in connection with natural place. We understand immediately that the orthogonal space of the Egyptians comprised this aspect, unifying the east-west course of the sun and the south-north direction of the Nile. Moreover the Egyptians over and over again reproduced their general image of heaven and earth in the floors, walls and ceilings of their temples. We have also reason to believe that the imagined four posts on which the sky rests, are a derivation from an archetypal building with a flat ceiling and a column at each corner. The understanding of the natural environment therefore does not necessarily *precede* building. The very act of building may become a means to this understanding, and the house may act as a "model" for the cosmic image, at last if a structural similarity is present. We thus realize the fundamental importance of architecture as a means to give man an existential foothold. The Nordic image of the cosmos as a house where the heavenly axis forms the ridge-beam and the *Irminsul* the northern of the two posts on which it rests, is also a projection of the structure of a simple archetypal house into the cosmic sphere[9]. And the Mediterranean image of a "cosmic cave", in obviously derived from natural caves as well as artificial caves such as the Roman Pantheon[10]. In this case, we find a reciprocal relationship between the natural and the man-made place.

The Romans possessed both the cave-image and the house-image, representing again a meeting of Mediterranean and Nordic elements. In the Pantheon two crossing axes are integrated in the cave-like rotunda, expressing thus that the world is both oriented and "round"[11]. On the urban level the Romans visualized the cosmic order by means of two main streets crossing each other at a right angle; the *cardo* running north-south and the *decumanus* east-west. This scheme has been known by many civilizations and was still alive in the Middle Ages[12]. The word "quarter" in connection with cities stems from this

52

division in four parts by the crossing axes. In the Middle Ages whole countries like Ireland and Iceland were divided in four parts. A Medieval world map from the 12th or 13th century, shows four symmetrically disposed continents, separated by seas and surrounded by a "mare magnum"[13]. We may also remind in this connection that the Christian basilica with transept is organized around a "crossing".

Whereas a cosmic order is visualized by means of spatial *organization*, characters are symbolized through formal *articulation*. Characters are more intangible than natural "things" and spatial relationships, and demand particular attention from the builder. In fact their concretization presupposes a language of symbolic forms (style). Such a language consists of basic elements which may be varied and combined in different ways. In other words it depends on systematic formal articulation. The decisive step in the development of a coherent formal language was taken by the Greeks. We have already pointed out that the Greek achievement consisted in a precise definition of different kinds of natural places, which were related to basic human characters. This definition meant something more than the meaningful dedication of a particular place to a particular god, although this might have been the first step[14]. Primarily it consisted in the building of symbolic structures, temples, which gave the intended character presence. The single temple may be understood as an individual member of a "family", just as the gods formed a family which symbolized the various roles and interactions of man on earth. The individual differences within the family were first of all expressed by the so called classical *Orders*, but also by variations within the Orders as well as combinations of traits from two or more Orders. Our theoretical knowledge

of the Orders goes back to the Roman architect Vitruvius. Vitruvius maintains that temples ought to be built in a different style according to their dedication, and proceeds by explaining the Orders in terms of human characters. The Doric column "furnishes the proportion of a man's body, its strength and beauty". The Ionic is characterized by "feminine slenderness", whereas the Corinthian "imitates the slight figure of a maiden"[15]. The articulation of Greek architecture therefore, cannot be understood in merely visual or aesthetic terms. Articulation meant making precise a particular character, and this character, simple or complex, determined every part of the building. In Renaissance architecture articulation was based on the "Vitruvian" tradition. Serlio calls the orders *opera di mano*, and implies that they represent different modes of human existence, while rustication was *opera di natura*, that is, a symbol of the original forces of the earth. As late as the eighteenth century the classical Orders formed the basis for an exceptionally sensitive treatment of symbolic characterization[16].

Architectural history, however, also knows other coherent symbolic languages. In Mediaeval European architecture, a systematic approach to architectural form served the purpose of symbolizing the ordered Christian cosmos[17]. As the Christian world is founded on the *spirit* as an existential reality, Mediaeval articulation aimed at "dematerialization", and negated the anthropomorphic classical Orders. Dematerialization was understood as a function of *light*, as a divine manifestation. We may therefore say that Mediaeval man "built" light, the most intangible of natural phenomena. Since then light has been a primary means of architectural characterization.

I addition to "forces", order, character

85. *Building light. Cappella Palatina, Palermo.*
86. *Building light. Amiens Cathedral.*

and light, the categories of natural understanding also comprise *time*, which is a basically different dimension. Time is not a phenomenon, but the order of phenomenal succession and change. Buildings and settlements, however, are static, apart from certain mobile elements of secondary importance. Nonetheless man has succeeded in "building" time, by translating basic temporal structures into spatial properties[18]. Primarily life is "movement", and as such it possesses "direction" and "rhythm". The *path* is therefore a fundamental existential symbol which concretizes the dimension of time. Sometimes the path leads to a meaningful goal, where the movement is arrested and time becomes permanence. Another basic symbol which concretizes the temporal dimension is therefore the *centre*. The archetypal buildings which visualize the concept of centre are the *Mal* and the enclosure, which often appear in combination. The *Mal* used by ancient civilizations was usually understood as an *axis mundi*. At the *acropolis*, *Mal* (hill) and enclosure (plateau) are unified. In ancient architecture we also usually find a *via sacra* which leads to the centre, and which is used for ritual re-enacting of "cosmic" events. In the Christian *basilica*, path (nave) and goal (altar) are united to symbolize the "Path of Salvation" of Christian doctrine. The basic phenomena of the urban environment, the *street* and the *square*, also belong to the categories of path and centre.

The man-made place visualizes, complements and symbolizes man's understanding of his environment. In addition it may also *gather* a number of meanings. Any true settlement is founded on gathering, and the basic forms are the farm, the agricultural village[19], the urban dwelling, and the town or city. All these places are essentially man-made or

87. *Path and goal. Belvedere, by Hildebrandt*
Vienna.
88. *Village. Pitigliano, southern Toscana.*
89. *Path and goal. S. Sabina, Rome.*

"artificial", but they fall into two distinct categories. The first two are directly related to the land, that is, they form part of a *particular* environment, and their structure is determined by this environment. In the urban dwelling and the town as a whole, instead, the direct relation to the natural environment is weakened or almost lost, and gathering becomes a bringing together of forms which have their roots in other localities. This is the *essential* property of the urban settlement. The main historical cities are therefore hardly found in places where a particular natural character is revealed (such as Delphi or Olympia), but somewhere *between* these places. Thereby they become comprehensive centres for a world which comprises a multitude of meanings. By moving the natural forces into the settlement, the forces were "domesticated", and the city became a fact "which helped to liberate man from the terror of the natural world with its dark powers and limiting laws"[20]. In a town such as Priene, the main gods are brought together and located, according to their particular nature, within the urban area, transforming thus the town into a meaningful *microcosmos*. But also the other buildings, public as well as private, are articulated by means of the classical Orders, and are thus related to the same system of meanings[21]. It goes without saying that the gathering function of the town determines a complex internal structure, an urban "inside". The same holds true for the house, which Alberti called a "small city". Through building, man-made places are created which possess their individual *genius loci*. This genius is determined by what is visualized, complemented, symbolized or gathered. In vernacular architecture the man-made genius loci ought to correspond closely to that of the natural place, in urban architecture,

instead, it is more comprehensive. The *genius loci* of a town, thus, ought to comprise the spirit of the locality to get "roots", but it should also gather contents of *general* interest, contents which have their roots elsewhere, and which have been moved by means of symbolization. Some of these contents (meanings) are so general that they apply to all places.

2. The Structure of Man-made Place

The term "man-made place" denotes a series of environmental levels, from villages and towns down to houses and their interiors. All these "places" begin their "presencing" (being) from the boundaries. We have already pointed out that the "presencing" thereby defined, in principle implies particular relationships to the ground and to the sky. A general introduction to the strucutre of man-made places therefore has to investigate these relationships with regard to the different environmental levels. *How* does a building stand and rise? (Evidently "standing" here comprises lateral extension and contact with the surroundings by means of openings). *How* is a settlement related to its environment, and *how* is its silhouette? Questions of this kind put the matter of structure in concrete terms, and give the phenomenology of architecture a realistic basis.

The distinctive quality of any man-made place is *enclosure*, and its character and spatial properties are determined by how it is enclosed. Enclosure, thus, may be more or less complete, openings and implied directions may be present, and the capacity of the place varies accordingly. Enclosure primarily means a distinct area which is separated from the surroundings by means of a built boundary. It may also be manifest in less strict form as a dense cluster of elements, where a continuous boundary is inferred

rather than positively present. An "enclosurc" may even be created by a mere change in the texture of the ground.

The cultural importance of defining an area which is qualitatively different from the surroundings, cannot be overestimated. The *temenos* is the archetypal form of meaningful space, and constitutes the point of departure for human settlement. In Japan, as has been shown by Günter Nitschke, basic cultural phenomena of various kinds were derived from the process of land demarkation[20]. The landmarks themselves were bundles of grass or reeds which were bound together in the middle to form a fan-like artifact which visualizes a separation of earth and heaven (bottom and top). A three-dimensional "cosmos" was thus defined within the given chaos. Nitschke furthermore points out that the very word for (enclosed) land, *shima*, was derived from the name of the land occupation mark, *shime*, and reminds us of a parallel connection of words in the German *Marke* (mark, sign) and *Mark* (land, e.g. Denmark)[23]. We may add that several Nordic terms for an enclosed "inside", *town, tun* (norw.), *týn* (czech) are derived from *Zaun*, that is, "fence", *vallis*, "valley", goes together with *vallum*, "wall", "palisade", and *vallus*, "pole"[24]. Indeed the enclosure began its presencing from the boundary.

The "how" of the enclosure depends upon the concrete properties of the boundaries. The boundaries determine the degree of enclosure ("openness") as well as the spatial direction, which are two aspects of the same phenomenon. When an opening is introduced in a centralized enclosure, an *axis* is created which implies longitudinal movement. We find such a combination of enclosure and longitudinality already at Stonehenge, where the "altar" is moved away from the geometrical centre in

58

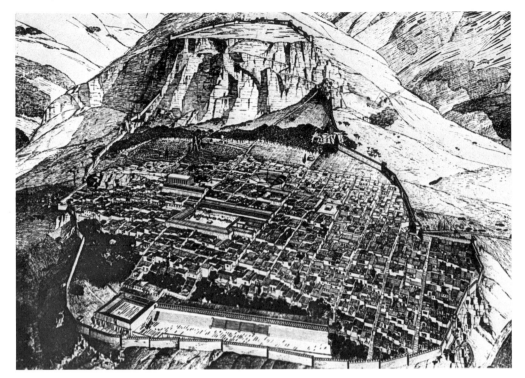

relation to the processional path which enters the area from the north-east[25]. The spatial structures developed during the history of architecture are always in one way or the other based on centralization and longitudinality and their combinations. The general significance of the concepts of centre and path is thus confirmed, but the particular ways of using these themes are to a high extent locally determined. Centralization and longitudinality are often emphasized by the upper boundary of the space, for instance by a hemispherical *dome* or a barrel *vault*. The ceiling may thus determine and visualize the internal spatial structure. In general the presence of a ceiling defines the particular kind of enclosures known as "interior space". When there is no ceiling, the sky acts as the upper boundary, and the space is, in spite of lateral boundaries, part of "exterior space". An enclosed space which is lit from above therefore offers a strange experience of being inside and outside at the same time.

The main urban elements are centres and paths. A square obviously functions as a centre and a street as a path. As such they are enclosures; their spatial identity in fact depends upon the presence of relatively continuous lateral boundaries. In addition to centre and path, we have introduced the word *domain* to denote a basic type of enclosure. An urban district is such a domain, and again we find that the presence of a boundary is of decisive importance. A district, thus, is either defined by conspicuous edges of some kind, or at least by a change in urben texture which implies a boundary. In combination, centres, paths and domains may form complex totalities which serve man's need for orientation. Of particular interest are the cases when a centre generates a domain, or "field", to use the word of Paolo Portoghesi[26]. This happens for

92. *Vault. S. Cataldo, Palermo.*
93. *Piazza. Il Campo, Siena.*
94. *Street. S. Gimignano, Toscana.*
95. *District. Pisticci, Basilicata.*

instance when a circular *piazza* is surrounded by a concentric system of streets. The properties of a "field" are hence determined by the centre, or by a regular repetition of structural properties. When several fields interact, a complex spatial structure results, of varying density, tension and dynamism[27].

Centre, path and domain are general and abstracts concepts, which translate the Gestalt principles into architectural terms. More concrete are certain archetypal configurations which are generated by these principles, or rather: which may be classified as centres, paths or domains. In architectural history, thus, we encounter centralized forms such as the *rotunda* and the regular polygons, which generate three-dimensional volumes. Le Corbusier still considered the sphere, the cube, the pyramid and the cylinder the elements of architectural form[26]. The basic longitudinal forms stem from an organization of space around a curved or straight line, and are equally important in buildings and towns. As built domains we may, finally, consider all kinds of clusters and groups of spaces or buildings. Whereas the cluster is based on simple proximity of the elements, and shows relatively indeterminate spatial relationships, the word "group" is mostly used to denote a regular, possibly geometrical, two- or three-dimensional spatial organization. The importance of the archetypal configurations is confirmed by the fact that towns and villages in any part of the world either belong to the centralized, the longitudinal or the clustered type. In German the types are known as *Rundling, Reihendorf* and *Haufendorf*[29]. Two spatial patterns of particular interest are the *grid* and the *labyrinth*. The grid is an "open", orthogonal infrastructure of paths, which may be filled in with

97. *Linear village. Caprarola, Lazio.*
98. *Cluster village with labyrinthine spaces. Ostuni, Puglia.*

buildings in different ways[30]. The labyrinth instead, is characterized by a lack of straight and continuous paths, and a high density. It is the traditional Arabic settlement pattern[31].

The *character* of a man-made place is to a high extent determined by its degree of "openness". The solidity or transparency of the boundaries make the space appear isolated or as part of a more comprehensive totality. We here return to the inside-outside relationship which constitutes the very essence of architecture. A place may thus be an isolated refuge, whose meaning is due to the presence of symbolic elements, it may communicate with an "understood" concrete environment, or be related to an ideal, imagined world. The last case is found in the "double-shell" spaces of late Baroque architecture, where the inside proper is embedded in a luminous zone which symbolizes the omnipresence of Divine Light[32]. Zones of transition may also be used to relate the internal structure of the place to the structure of the natural or man-made environment. We may in this context again remind of Robert Venturi, who says: "Architecture occurs at the meeting of interior and exterior forces of use and space"[33]. Evidently this meeting is expressed in the *wall*, and in particular in the *openings* which connect the two "domains".

A man-made place, however, is something more than a space with a varying degree of openness. As a *building*, it stands on the ground, and rises towards the sky. The character of the place is to a high extent determined by *how* this standing and rising is concretized. This also holds true for entire settlements, such as towns. When a town pleases us because of its distinct character, it is usually because a majority of its buildings are related to the earth and the sky in the same way; they seem to

99. *Double-shell structure. In der Wies by* *Zimmermann.*

100. *On the ground under the sky. Temple of* *Heaven, Peking.*
101. *"Gerüst". Open barn in western Norway.*

express a common form of life, a common way of being on the earth. Thus they constitute a *genius loci* which allows for human identification.

The "how" of a building comprises a general and particular aspect. In general any building possesses a concrete structure (*Gerüst*) which may be described in formal-technical terms, and in particular an individual articulation of this structure. An archetypal building in this sense is a house whose primary structure consists of a ridge-beam carried by a (gabled) post at either end. Such a house possesses a clear, easily imageable order, which in ancient times helped man to gain a feeling of security. This fact is confirmed by the etymology and relationship of the terms which denote the various parts of the structure. The word "ridge", thus, in general means the crest of something, and in particular a chain of mountains. The corresponding Norvegian word *ås* means "hill" and "god" as well as the ridge of the house. The German *First* has many connotations, among which *Forst* is particularly interesting, as it denotes an enclosed area in general[34]. Of primary importance in the structure is the point where the horizontal and vertical members are connected, the "gable". In the Middle Ages the German world *Giebel* meant gable as well as the poles of the sky[35]. Here we return again to the relationship between house and cosmic order, which was discussed above. What is important to stress in this context however, is that the meaning of a building is related to its structure. Meaning and character cannot be interpreted in purely formal or aesthetic terms, but are, as we have already pointed out, intimately connected with *making*. Heidegger in fact defines the "method" of art as *ins-werk-setzen* (to "set-into-work")[36]. This is the meaning of architectural concretization: *to set a place into work*, in

102. *Making. Clay houses in Tunis.*
103. *Making. Loft at Kleivi, Aamotsdal, Norway.*

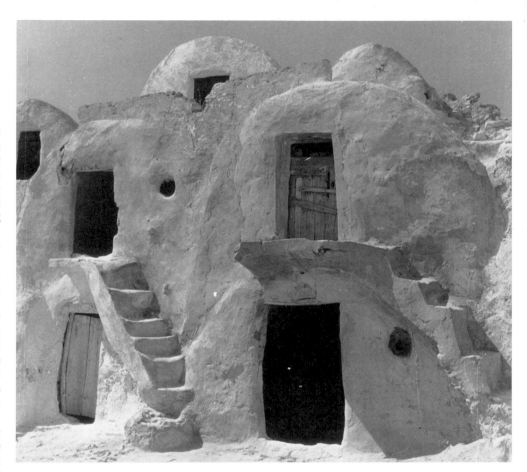

the sense of concrete building. The character of a work of architecture is therefore first of all determined by the kind of construction used; whether it is skeletal, open and transparent (potentially or in fact), or massive and enclosed. And secondly by the making as such: binding, joining, erecting etc. These processes express how the meaning of the work becomes a "thing". Thus Mies van der Rohe said: "Architecture starts when you put two bricks carefully upon each other".

Making is an aspect of *articulation*. The other aspect is "form". Articulation determines *how* a building stands and rises, and *how* it receives light. The word "stand" denotes its relationship to the earth, and "rise" its relationship to the sky. Standing is concretized through the treatment of the *base* and the *wall*. A massive and perhaps concave base and accentuated horizontals "tie" the building to the ground, whereas an emphasis on the vertical direction tends to make it "free". Vertical lines and forms express an active relationship to the sky and a wish for receiving light. Verticalism and religious aspiration have in fact always gone together. In the wall, thus, earth and sky meet, and the way man "is" on earth is concretized by the solution of this meeting. Some buildings are "ground-hugging", others rise freely, and in others again we find a meaningful equilibrium. Such an equilibrium is for instance found in the Doric temple, where the details and the proportions of the columns express that they stand *and* rise. By means of subtle variations in the treatment, the Greeks could express significant nuances within the general equilibrium[37]. In the first Hera temple in Paestum the strong *entasis* of the columns as well as other details brings us close to the earth, in accordance with the character of the goddess. In the temple of Apollo in

104. *Making. Stone building in Montepulciano.*
105. *Standing and rising. Street in Innsbruck.*
106. *Standing and rising. Temple in Selinunte.*

Corinth, instead, *entasis* is entirely a-bolished to express the more abstract, intellectual strength of the god.

A meaningful relationship between horizontals and verticals also depends on the form of the *roof*. Flat or sloping roofs, gables, domes and pointed spires express different relations to earth and sky, and determine the general character of the building. In his houses, Frank Lloyd Wright wanted simultaneously to express belonging to the earth and "freedom" in space[38]. Thus he composed the building of planes of "infinite" extension parallel to the ground, but introduced a vertical core as well as low hipped roofs to give it an anchorage. The (horizontal) freedom in space is also concretized by an opening up of the walls by means of bands of glass. The wall is no longer there to enclose space, but rather to direct it and to achieve a unification of inside and outside.

In general *openings* serve to concretize different inside-outside relationships. "Holes" in a massive wall give emphasis to enclosure and interiority, whereas the filling in of a skeletal wall by large surfaces of glass "de-materialize" the building and create an interaction between exterior and interior. Openings also receive and transmit *light*, and are therefore main determinants of architectural character. Large-scale environments are often characterized by particular types of windows end doors, which thereby become *motifs* which condense and visualize the local character. Finally, it ought to be mentioned that material and colour may contribute decisively to characterization. Stone, brick and wood are different "presences" which express the way buildings "are" on earth. In Florence, for instance, rusticated stone was used to concretize a rational, "built" environment possessing "classical" substance and order. In Siena, instead, the use of continuous

107. *Roof as formal factor. Gateway at Göttweig by Hildebrandt.*
108. *"French" window. Paris.*
109. *Built architecture. Palazzo Strozzi, Florence.*

110. *Hole and massivity. Farm house in Bardonecchia, Piedmont.*
111. *Continuous architecture. Street in Siena.*

"de-materialized" brick surfaces create an atmosphere of Mediaeval spirituality. It goes without saying that the choice of material and colour is intimately linked with "making" in general, although a certain independence may be meaningful, as when built walls are painted in colours which have a mere characterizing function. A "freedom" of this kind is obviously more common in enclosed interior spaces, where the direct contact with the environment is weaker, and where character therefore implies a gathering of "distant" meanings.

It would in this context carry us too far to develop a systematic typology of man-made places. We have already mentioned the farm, the village, the urban house and the town as primary categories. A further differentiation ought to be based on the various "building-tasks" which make up a human settlement[39]. It ought to be repeated, however, that man-made places form a hierarchy of environmental levels. The settlement as a whole is externally related to a natural or cultural landscape by which it is contained. Internally the settlement contains subplaces such as squares, streets and districts ("quarters"). These sub-places again contain and are defined by buildings serving different purposes. Within the buildings we find the interior spaces, in the common sense of the word. The interior contains artifacts which define an innermost goal (such as the altar of a church, or the table in Trakl's poem). The structural properties of the various levels as well as their formal interrelations, concretize the "form of life" as a whole, in an individual as well as a social sense. We shall later introduce the concepts of "private" and "public" to arrive at a fuller understanding of the place as a "living" totality.

Structurally, orientation and identification means the experience of man-made place within man-made place. The different "insides" are "known" in accordance with their structural properties. In most settlements in fact we find that the naming of the urban spaces reflects the existence of distinct man-made places which have a structurally determined identity[40]. The man-made *genius loci* depends on *how* these places are in terms of space and character, that is, in terms of organization and articulation.

3. The Spirit of Man-Made Place

Our discussion of the phenomena of man-made place has uncovered several basic types of man-made factors, which helped our understanding of the structure of man-made place, as well as its relationship to natural place. Any concrete situation is distinguished by a particular combination of these factors which constitute the *genius loci* as an integrated totality. There are man-made places where the variety and mystery of the natural forces are strongly felt, there are places where the manifestation of an abstract general order has been the main intention, and there are places where force and order have found a comprehensible equilibrium. We thus return to the categories of "romantic", "cosmic" and "classical". Although these categories are abstractions which are hardly concretized in "pure" form, they express concrete tendencies, and therefore serve a general understanding of the spirit of place. Any concrete situation may in fact be understood as a synthesis of these basic categories. Using the word "architecture" to denote the concretization of man-made places in general, we may hence talk about "romantic architecture", "cosmic architecture", and "classical architecture".

Romantic architecture

As "romantic" we designate an architecture distinguished by multiplicity and variety. It cannot easily be understood in logical terms, but seems irrational and "subjective" (although the inherent meanings may be of general value). Romantic architecture is characterized by a strong "atmosphere", and may appear "phantastic" and "mysterious", but also "intimate" and "idyllic". In general it is distinguished by a live and dynamic character, and aims at "expression"[41]. Its forms seem to be a result of "growth" rather than organization, and resemble the forms of living nature.

Romantic space is topological rather than geometrical. On the urban level this means that the basic configurations are the dense and indeterminate cluster and the "free" and varied row. The urban spaces are distinguished by irregular enclosure, and contain functions in a general way, without aiming at regular, defined distribution. "Strong" romantic spaces and configurations demand a continuous but geometrically indeterminate boundary. In relation to the surroundings the romantic settlement is identified by the proximity of its elements, or by general enclosure.

The "atmosphere" and expressive character of romantic architecture is obtained by means of formal complexity and contradiction. Simple, intelligible volumes are avoided and transformed into transparent, skeletal structures, where the *line* becomes a symbol of force and dynamism. Although the construction as such may be logical, it usually appears irrational due to the multiplication of members, variation in detailing, and introduction of "free" ornament. The outside-inside relationship is usually complex, and the romantic building and settlement are characterized by a serrate and "wild" silhouette. Light is used to emphasize variety and atmosphere rather than

comprehensible elements. Usually it has a strong local quality, which may be stressed through the application of particular colours.

The Mediaeval town is the romantic settlement *par excellence*, particularly in Central Europe, where classical influence (natural or historical) is less strongly felt than for instance in Italy. The Mediaeval town makes its presence visible in towers and spires, and its spaces are characterized by the pointed gables of the houses, as well as by rich irrational detail. According to the natural environment the character varies, from the "wild-romantic" Alpine settlement to the idyllic interaction of buildings and surroundings in Northern Germany and Denmark. In Innsbruck, for instance, the houses are heavy and massive down at the ground with low and mysterious arcades, but they rise towards the sky with stepped and undulating gables. In a northern town like Celle, the gabled houses become skeletal and are transformed into an atmospheric play of colours. In Norway, finally, the Nordic character culminates in the eminently romantic structures of the stave-church and the *loft,* and in the white-painted houses which concretize the luminosity of the Nordic summer night. The summer night in fact became part of man's built environment when the colour white was invented. Before, the houses were dark, reflecting the mystery of the winter sky, which is also the light of the stave-church interior. In the stave-church it makes sense to talk about "dark light", as a Divine manifestation.

In more recent architecture, the romantic character is fully present and wonderfully interpreted in the *Art Nouveau*. Later it appears, in a different key, in the "forest" architecture of Alvar Aalto, differently again, in the works of Hugo Häring, who aimed at making an

112. *Romantic architecture. Dinkelsbühl.*
113. *Romantic architecture. Street in Celle.*
114. *Romantic architecture. Dark and white-painted lofts at Tjønntveit, Numedal, Norway.*

115. *Romantic architecture. Own house by Guimard, Paris.*

organhaft architecture, that is, buildings which are "organs" to the functions they serve, like the organs of our body. Thereby Häring gave the romantic approach an actual definition[42]. In general, the multiplicity and variety of romantic architecture is unified by a basic *Stimmung*, which corresponds to particular formative principles. Romantic architecture is therefore eminently *local*.

Cosmic architecture

As "cosmic" we designate an architecture distinguished by uniformity and "absolute" order. It can be understood as an integrated logical system, and seems rational and "abstract", in the sense of transcending the individual concrete situation. Cosmic architecture is distinguished by a certain lack of "atmosphere", and by a very limited number of basic characters. It is neither "phantastic" nor "idyllic", words which denote direct human participation, but remains aloof. Its forms are static rather than dynamic, and seems to be the revelation of a "hidden" order, rather than the result of concrete composition. It aims at "necessity" rather than expression.

Cosmic space is strictly geometrical and is usually concretized as a regular grid, or as a cross of orthogonal axes (*cardo-decumanus*). It is uniform and isotropic, although its directions are qualitatively different. That is, the qualitative differences are not expressed as such, but are absorbed by the system. Cosmic space, however, also knows an "inversion" which we may call "labyrinthine space". The labyrinth does not possess any defined or goal-oriented direction, it rests in itself without beginning and end[43]. Basically it is therefore "cosmic", although it seems to belong to another spatial family than the grid. "Strong" cosmic spaces demand a clear visualization of the system. In

116. Cosmic architecture. Decumanus at Gerasa.
117. Cosmic architecture. Courtyard of the Mirimah mosque, Istanbul.

118. Labyrinthine world. Village at Tuti island, Khartoum.
119. Open grid. Massachusetts avenue, Cambridge, Mass.

relation to the surroundings it may remain "open", as it does not take the local microstructure into consideration.

The character of cosmic architecture is also distinguished by "abstraction". Thus it shuns sculptural presence, and tends to dematerialize volumes and surfaces by means of "carpet-like" decoration (mosaic, glazed tiles etc.), or by the introduction of intricate geometrical webs. Horizontals and verticals do not represent active forces, but are put in a simple juxtaposition as manifestations of the general order.

In Islamic architecture the cosmic approach finds its major manifestation. The Islamic city, thus, consists of a combination of geometrical and labyrinthine space. Whereas the main public buildings are based on an orthogonal grid (Mosque, Medrese, etc.), the residential quarters are labyrinthine, a fact which expresses the desert origin of Islamic culture as well as the social structure of the Arabic settlement[44], which, after all, are two aspects of the same totality. The "abstract" presence of horizontals and verticals (the Minaret), concretizes the general order, and gives a first suggestion of the cosmic character. In interior space this character becomes the manifestation of an ideal world, a paradise of white, green, and blue, that is, the colours of pure light, vegetation and water, which represents the goal of man's desert voyage.

But cosmic architecture may be interpreted in other ways. We have already described the absolute systems of the Egyptians and the Romans. The latter is of particular interest in our context, as it was brought along and implanted everywhere regardless of the local circumstances. In general the Romans therby expressed that every individual place forms part of a comprehensive cosmic (and political!) system which it has to obey. In Roman architecture this

order penetrated all levels, down to the interior space of individual buildings. Thus the Roman conquest of the world happened as the manifestation of a preestablished cosmic order, "in agreement with the gods"[45].

In modern times, the image of a cosmic order has degenerated into spatial systems which concretize political, social or economic structures. The grid-iron plans of American cities, for instance, do not express any cosmological concept, but make an "open" world of opportunities manifest. This world is open horizontally as well as vertically. Whereas the community expands horizontally, the success of the individual is indicated by the hight of the building erected on the standard lot. Although the grid-iron thus possesses a certain "freedom", it hardly allows for the concretization of a distinct *genius loci*. Spatial systems of the cosmic type therefore ought to form part of more complex totalities.

Classical architecture

As "classical" we designate an architecture distinguished by imageability and articulate order. Its organization can be understood in logical terms, whereas its "substance" asks for empathy. It therefore appears "objective", in the double sense of the word. Classical architecture is characterized by concrete presence, and each element is a distinct "personality". Its forms are neither static nor dynamic, but pregnant with "organic life". They seem the result of a conscious com-position of individual elements, and give man simultaneously a sense of belonging and freedom.

Classical space unifies topological and geometrical traits. The individual building may possess a strict geometrical order, which forms the basis for its identity[46], whereas the organization of several buildings is topological. A certain "democratic" freedom is thereby

120. *Classical architecture. Detail from the Propylaea, Athens.*

121. *Classical architecture. The acropolis, Athens.*

expressed. Classical architecture is thus distinguished by the absence of a general, dominant system, and its space may be defined as an additive grouping of individual places. Whereas the classical landscape was understood as a *veduta*, classical architecture is described by means of *perspective*. In relation to the surroundings the classical settlement appears as a distinct, characteristic presence.

This presence is achieved by means of plastic articulation. In the classical building all the parts have their individual identity, at the same time as they condense, explain and perhaps differentiate the general character of the whole. Each character forms part of a "family" of characters, which are deliberately related to human qualities. In classical architecture the original forces are thus "humanized", and present themselves as individual participants in a comprehensive, meaningful world. The logic of construction is interpreted as an interaction of active and passive members, and the classical building therefore appears "built" in a direct and intelligible way. Light, finally, is used to give emphasis to the plastic presence of the parts and the whole by means of a play of light and shadow which "models" the form.

We have already made several references to Greek architecture, and should only add that it, in its developed Classical phase, represents the archetype of classical architecture. Throughout history the harmonious and meaningful equilibrium of Greek buildings and settlements has remained an ideal, which has been revived in ever new contexts. In Roman architecture the classical component was strong, but it faded away towards late Antiquity, when plastic presence was substituted by de-materialization and the symbolic "building" of light[47]. In the Florentine Renaissance, however, certain

122. *Temple of Nike, Athens.*
123. *Renaissance. Ospedale degli Innocenti, Florence by Brunelleschi.*

aspects of classical architecture reappeared. Again we find the wish for giving the buildings individual plastic presence and anthropomorphous characterization, in combination with simple, intelligible construction. We also find that spatial organization was understood as an addition of "independent" units. What is different form Classical Greek architecture, is the coordination of all parts within a comprehensive, homogeneous space, a concept which has cosmic implications and reflects a belief in a "harmonious" universe. The development of homogeneous space, however, did not prevent meaningful spatial differentiation[48].

In our own time the classical attitude has played an important part. Thus Le Corbusier wrote: "Architecture is the masterly, correct and magnificent play of volumes brought together in light. Our eyes are made to see forms in light; light and shade reveal these forms; cubes, cones, spheres, cylinders and pyramids are the great primary forms...; the image of these is distinct... and without ambiguity"[49]. Le Corbusier evidently wanted plastic presence and intelligibility, but a certain "abstraction" is also felt, which differs from the "organic" approach of Greek architecture. The true presence which brings the world "close", was in fact hardly understood by early modern architecture.

Complex architecture
Romantic, cosmic and classical architecture are archetypes of man-made place. As they are related to the basic categories of natural understanding, they help us to interpret the *genius loci* of any particular settlement. Being types, however, they hardly appear in pure form, but participate in various kinds of syntheses. In the history of European architecture two such syntheses are of particular interest: The Gothic cathedral

and the Baroque garden-palace. The Gothic cathedral belongs to the romantic Mediaeval town, but transcends its attachment in the natural environment. In the interior of the cathedral atmospheric light is translated into a Divine manifestation, and the systematically subdivided structure represents a visualization of the ordered cosmos described by scholastic philosophy[50].

The cathedral therefore unites romantic and cosmic qualities, and through its transparent walls the locally interpreted existential meanings of Christianity were transmitted to the town, whose everyday life-world thereby got a cosmic dimension. In the Baroque garden-palace we find a different kind of synthesis[51]. Here the cosmic dimension is not represented by light as a symbol of the spirit and by a structural system which rises up to receive this light, but by a horizontally extended geometrical network of paths which concretizes the absolutist pretentions of the Sovereign located at the centre of the system. The centre is moreover used to divide the "world" in two halves: a man-made, urban environment on one side, and "infinitely" extended nature on the other. Close to the centre nature appears as a cultural landscape (*parterre*), further away it becomes more "natural" (*bosquet*), to end in a "wilderness". In the Baroque garden-palace, thus, man-made and natural place are united to form a comprehensive whole, with romantic and cosmic implications as well as a built form of classical derivation in the palace itself[52].

As the urban environment is based on gathering, it usually offers many possibilities of identification. It is therefore easier to feel "at home" in a foreign city than in a foreign landscape. The *genius loci* of the human settlement in fact represents a microcosmos, and cities differ in what they gather. In some, the forces of the earth are strongly felt, in others the ordering power of the sky, others again have the presence of humanized nature, or are saturated with light. All cities, however, have to possess something of all these categories of meaning to make *urban dwelling* possible. Urban dwelling consists in the assuring experience of being simultaneously located and open to the world, that is: located in the natural *genius loci* and open to the world through the gathering of the man-made *genius-loci*[53].

1. Image

Few places exert such a fascination as Prague. Other cities may be grander, more charming, or more "beautiful". Prague, however, seizes you and remains with you as hardly any other place.
"Prague does not let go – either of you or of me. This little mother has claws. There is nothing for it but to give in or – . We would have to set it on fire from two sides, at the Vyšehrad and at the Hradčany, only thus could we free ourselves"[1].
The fascination of Prague resides first of all in a strong sense of mystery. Here you have the feeling that it is possible to penetrate ever deeper into things. Streets, gates, courtyards, staircases lead you into an endless "inside". Over and over again this theme comes out in the literature of Prague; in Kafka it forms the ground for his images and characters, and in Gustav Meyrink's novel "The Golem", the unfathomable spaces of the Old Town become the bearing theme. These spaces do not only lose themselves horizontally, but also *under* the ground of everyday life. The symbolic content of "The Golem" is thus centred on an empty room which has a window but no door[2]. To reach it one has to go through a subterranean labyrinth and find an opening in the floor. The same *we* have to do if we want to understand the *genius loci* of Prague. Here all houses have deep roots in layers of history, and from these roots they rise up, having individual names which suggest a legendary past. Architecturally these roots are expressed by heavy and massive ground-floors, low arcades and deeply-set openings. Walking around in old Prague, one always has the feeling of being "down" in spaces that are mysterious and frightening, but also warm and protective.
This closeness to the earth, however, is only one aspect of its *genius loci*. Prague

126. *Winter night in Prague.*

127. *Old street in Prague.*
128. *Tÿn church from the Old Town Square.*
129. *The "Prague view". The Small Town across the Vltava.*

is also known as the "city of hundred steeples"; and its architecture is in fact saturated with vertical movement. The urban spaces are focused on towers and spires, and the dormers and gables of the old houses accompany us everywhere. Simple vertical accents do not seem to be enough in Prague, and the mediaeval steeples of churches, townhalls and bridge-towers are surrounded by clusters of pointed spires. In the Baroque churches, the vertical movement seems transformed into flames which rise toward the sky. Thus the mysteries of the earth find their counterpart in heavenly aspiration.

The strength of Prague as a place depends first of all on the felt presence of the *genius loci* throughout; practically every old house is simultaneously ground-hugging and aspiring. In some buildings, however, the local character is given particular emphasis, and it is very significant that these buildings serve as foci to the different parts of the city. In the Old Town, thus, the Tÿn church with its clustered Gothic steeples rises above the low arcades of the main square, whereas the Small Town on the other side of the river is dominated by the Baroque dome and tower of St. Nicholas, which grow out of a massive and heavy basement. But this is not all; also as un urban totality Prague is distinguished by the contrast between earth and sky. Thus the steep hill of the Hradčany castle contrasts with the horizontally extended cluster of the Old Town, and the castle itself gathers the local character in its long horizontal lines over which the Cathedral of St. Vitus rises vertically towards the sky. This last juxtaposition is the crowning motif of the famous "Prague view": the vertically climbing Small Town seen over the horizontal expanse of the Vltava. Is there any other city in the world where the character is thus

130. *Charles Bridge from above.*

131. *Prague in winter.*
132. *Diagrammatic map of Bohemia.*
133. *Prague in the landscape.*

concretized in one single *veduta* which comprises all environmental levels from the landscape down to the articulation of the individual building?

The two main parts of Prague, the Old Town down on the flat land within the curve of the river, and the Small Town and castle hill on the other side, are linked by the Charles Bridge. In Prague indeed "the bridge gathers the earth as landscape around the stream", but it also gathers what man has contributed to the place, as a townscape of unique quality. Landscape and townscape are thus unified; the "Prague view" is in fact saturated with gardens, without reducing however, the figural character of the man-made place. From the bridge the whole is experienced as an *environment* in the full sense of the word; the bridge constitutes the very centre of this world, which evidently gathers so many meanings.

The Charles Bridge is a work of art in its own right; its broken and partly curved movement collects the streets on either side, and its towers and statues form a counterpoint to the horizontal series of arches across the river.

Men and women crossing dark bridges,
past the statues of saints
with their faint glimmer of light.

Clouds drifting over grey skies,
past churches
with misty towers.

A man leaning over the parapet
and gazing into the river at evening
his hands resting on ancient stone[3].

The strength of Prague as a place therefore also depends on its imageability. Its secrets do not make us get lost, the unfathomable insides always form part of a meaningful general structure which ties them together as the facets of a mysteriously glimmering gem. Like a gem, indeed, Prague changes with the

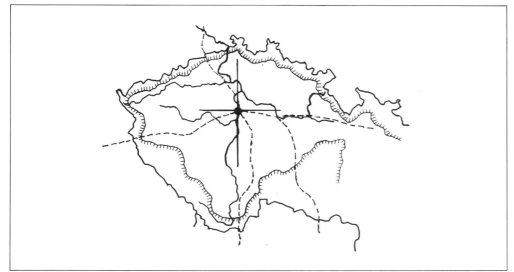

weather, the time of the day and the seasons. Only rarely, however, the sun gives its buildings their full plasticity. Mostly the light is filtered through clouds, the towers become "misty" and the sky is hidden. And still, this does not mean a loss of presence. In Prague what is hidden seems even more real that what is directly perceived. The presence of the invisible is used by Kafka at the very beginning of "The Castle" to intonate the basic atmosphere of the novel. In Prague, thus, we encounter a particular kind of "microstructure"; a structure whose richness does not only reside in the micro scale, but in what is dimly suggested. In the night the street lights make this characteristic particularly evident. The illumination is not continuous and even; strongly lit and dark zones alternate, and make us remember the times when a street lamp created a place.

The architecture of Prague is cosmopolitan without ever losing its local flavour. Romanesque, Gothic, Renaissance, Baroque, *Jugend* and "Cubist" buildings live together as if they were variations on the same theme[4]. Mediaeval and classical forms are transformed to make the same local character manifest; motifs from the Slavic east, the Germanic north, the Gallic west and the Latin south meet in Prague and blend into a singular synthesis. The catalyst which made this process possible was the *genius loci* proper, which, as we have already suggested, consists in a particular sense of earth and sky. In Prague classical architecture becomes romantic, and romantic architecture absorbs the classical characters to endow the earth with a particular kind of surreal humanity. Both become cosmic, not in the sense of abstract order, but as spiritual aspiration. Evidently Prague is one of the great meeting-places where a multitude of meanings are gathered.

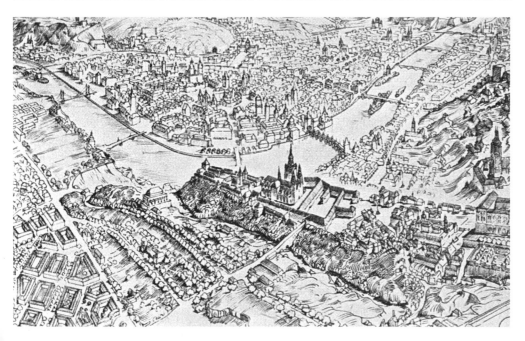

2. Space

If we take a look at the map of Central Europe, the particular location of Prague is immediately evident. Not only is Prague situated at the centre of Bohemia, but Bohemia is also in the very middle of those countries which for centuries have constituted the complex and turbulent core of the Western world. The central location of Bohemia is emphasized by the almost continuous range of mountains and hills which surround the area. A kind of basin is thus created, although the land has a very varied surface relief and natural "content". The feeling of a boundary is strengthened by the vegetation; the fertile interior is enclosed by forests which accompany the mountains. In general Bohemia appears as a rolling and friendly countryside, but it contains many surprises such as wild and strange rock formations. From the south to the north the country is divided in two halves by the river Vltava (Moldau) and its continuation, the Labe (Elbe). In the past it was difficult to cross these rivers; only one ford had a convenient, central location. Here the ancient road from Ucraina and Poland crossed the Vltava and continued into Germany. At the ford, it met the road which led from Austria in the south, to Saxony and Prussia. A very important node was thus created, and already in the sixth century it gave rise to a settlement which should become the city of Prague.

The geographical properties of Bohemia made the country predestined to become a cosmopolitan centre. A similar role is played by Switzerland, but here the geographical definition is less distinct, and a primary nodal point is lacking. In Europe, with its many ethnic groups and civilizations, a meeting place necessarily means problems. Hardly any other European country, in fact, has had a more complex and difficult history than

Bohemia. It is obviously due to the clear geographical definition that the first permanent settlers, the Czechs, have been able to survive. Possessing their own limited world, they have for centuries resisted the pressure of the neighbours, who managed, however, to occupy the zones along the border[5]. Throughout history, thus, Bohemia has been both a meeting place and an ethnic "island" with its own distinct identity. The double nature of the country is a main reason for its very particular character. As an ethnic island it has always conserved its roots in the proper soil, and as a meeting place it has been exposed to the impact of the entire European culture. The fact that the foreign import has always been transformed when it came to Bohemia proves the strength of its people and its *genius loci*.

At Prague the rolling landscape of central Bohemia is condensed to form a particularly beautiful configuration. Along the large bend of the Vltava an extended hill rises which visualizes the curve of the river. The hill and the river are opposed but complementary forces, which make nature become alive with expressive power. Within the curve, opposite the hill, the land opens up in horizontal expanse before it starts to rise gently towards the south-east. At either end of the river – bend two marked isolated hills give definition to the area. The two halves of this extraordinary landscape were linked by a ford, a little to the north of the present Charles Bridge. On the left bank at the height of the ford, there is a valley which makes it possible to reach the castle hill and the lands towards the west. As predestined for an urban settlement was this site, not only because of its beauty, but because it satisfied the three basic demands of the early Middle Ages: the flat plain for a market place, the hill for a protecting castle, and the ford for communication and commerce.

In the ninth century the Czech Přemyslids built the first castle and in 890 the first historically known Czech king Bořivoj added the first church in Bohemia, which was dedicated to the Holy Virgin. The Czech word for castle, *hrad*, determined its name, Hradčany. The oldest report on Prague stems from 965, and was written by an Arabic-Jewish merchant Ibrahim Ibn Jakub. He tells that the town was built of stone and mortar, and that it was the richest place in the whole country. The population already comprised groups of German, Jewish and Latin origin. About 1200, Romanesque Prague had 25 churches, many monasteries and a stone bridge. Shortly afterwards the different settlements on the right bank were gathered within a city wall, and in 1232-34 the Old Town (Staré Město) was a legal reality. The Small Town (Malá Strana) on the left bank was founded in 1257, and about 1300 the settlement on the Hradčany got urban rights. A fourth city, the New Town (Nové Město) was added around the Old Town by Charles IV in 1348.

Already in the Middle Ages, thus, the spatial structure of Prague had been defined. The city had found its form in accordance with the natural situation. First of all it consists of three parts: the dense settlement down on the plain, the dominant castle on the hill above, and the river as a separating and connecting element between them. We have seen that this structure is still alive, and it becomes immediately evident when the place is experienced from its centre, the bridge. During the course of history the basic juxtaposition has been interpreted and enriched by the buildings of successive generations. The verticalism of the hill has found an echo in the steeples and towers of the town, and the attachment to the earth of the latter is reflected in the horizontal expanse of the castle. In this way Prague has become an integrated totality, where the particular relationship between horizontal and vertical, between "above" and "below" serves as the unifying force. When we walk around in the streets or along the river, the relationship between town and castle is experienced in ever new variations. During history this juxtaposition has had its particular meaning. Whereas the castle in the Mediaeval cities meant protection and security, in Prague it often represented a threat. On the Hradčany lived the rulers, who, at several crucial occasions, spoke another language and professed another faith than the majority of the inhabitants. The Thirty Years war in fact started in Prague with a revolt, when the infuriated crowd threw the Imperial governors out of the windows of the castle, according to an "old Czech custom".

Prague's growth into an industrial capital from the nineteenth century on, has brought about some changes which weaken the general urban structure. The clear delimitation of the Old and New Towns by means of city walls is gone, although the street pattern still gives them a certain spatial identity. The urban sprawl around the old core has impaired the figural character of the city, although the generous extension of Charles IV for centuries allowed Prague to grow inside its walls. Certain urban districts have disappeared, first of all the Ghetto which was situated in the north-western part of the Old Town. It was one of the most characteristic parts of the city, but because of its slum-like conditions it was torn down after 1893. Today the Small Town and the Hradčany best preserve the general structure; here the habitat is still surrounded by green, such as the Petřin and Letná

parks at either end of the castle, and even the city-walls are in part standing.

The interior urban spaces of Prague still to a high extent follow the pattern laid out in the Middle Ages. The old thoroughfare between East and West serves as a backbone, connecting the main foci of the Old and the Small Towns. As the visitor walks along this path, the history of Prague becomes alive, and gradually a rich and coherent image of the city is formed in his mind. It starts at the Powder-Tower (1475), which is what remains of the old city wall. The tower is richly ornate and was obviously intended as something more than a mere "functional" city-gate. Inside the gate a well conserved street, the Celetná leads to the Old Town Square (Staroměstské Náměstí). On the way it passes the oldest part of the town, the *Týn*, where the merchants throughout the centuries paid duty for their goods. The *Týn* is a large courtyard enclosed by buildings whose Mediaeval core is covered with Renaissance and Baroque façades. The Old Town Square is a large "ring", subdivided by the centrally placed Town Hall and adjacent buildings into a larger and a smaller part. It is surrounded by relatively narrow gabled houses, and dominated by the twin towers of the Týn church (1365ff). From the Small Square the path continues rather tortuously to the Charles Bridge (1357ff). The bridge is a space in its own right, having Gothic towers with gates at either end and being lined with statues. Its bent movement is due to the fact that it was partly built over the foundations of the old Judith-bridge (1158-72) which collapsed in 1342. Upon entering the Small Town another splendid, well-conserved street, the Mostecká leads up to the Small Town Square (Malostranské Náměstí) which repeats the "ring" pattern of the Old Town Square. Here, however, the

136. *The Powder-Tower.*
137. *The Týn courtyard.*
138. *The Old Town Square.*

church of St. Nicholas (1703-52) with adjacent Jesuit college takes up the centre, whereas the Town Hall is situated along the eastern side of the square. Another beautiful, steeply rising street, the Nerudová, connects the Small Town with the Hradčany. Actually the Nerudova continues towards the west under the castle; a steep hill however leads up to the Hradčany Square, which is situated between the castle proper and the castle town. From here the view of Prague is splendid; the hill and the arch of the river embrace the Old Town, which responds with its towers and steeples. Under the castle the Small Town steps rhythmically down towards the river with its dense cluster of houses and gardens. But our walk is not finished before we enter the castle. Here a cluster of courtyards and lanes represents a variation on the spatial themes of the city itself, and in the centre we find the splendid interior space of the Cathedral (1344ff).

Whereas the urban structure of the Old Town and the Small Town follows the early Mediaeval pattern, the New Town was deliberately planned. As it forms a wide belt around the eastern side of the Old Town, a radial lay-out was natural. Rather than being a centralized structure in its own right, it prepares for the almost circular enclosure of the Old Town[6]. The radial pattern is visualized by three large squares which in the past served as hay market, horse market and cattle market, respectively. The middle one, St. Venceslaus' Square (Vaclavské Naměstí) has the rather unusual length of 680 mt., and functions today as a kind of "main street" for the whole city. Up till our time the New Town remained quite open and green. Thus the Old Town always was the dense core of the whole conurbation.

When the old city walls were torn down in the nineteenth century, streets were

139. *Old house in the Charles street.*

140. *The Old Town bridge tower.*
141. *On the Charles Bridge.*
142. *The Mostecká with St. Nicholas in the Small Town.*

laid out according to the old pattern and new bridges were built to connect the main streets on both sides of the river. Although the Charles Bridge is no longer alone, it has maintained its focal importance, and the new bridges are well integrated in the "organic" path structure of the city.

The secondary streets of old Prague have the character of narrow, twisting alleys. As such they possess an outspoken continuity, but many small-squares are introduced as subordinate urban foci. In the Old Town it is very common that the houses may be entered from two sides (*Durchhäuser*). It is therefore possible to walk through certain sections of the town without using the streets. This particular spatial property contributes decisively to the "mysterious" quality of Prague. The internal passages often lead through several courtyards which are mostly surrounded by characteristic balconies (*pavlač*). In the past these balconies were the stage where the colourful popular life took place. Spatially they served as a semi-public transition between the urban outside and the private interior of the houses. We understand, thus, that the feeling typical for Prague, that one might penetrate ever deeper inside is determined by its spatial structure. In the Small Town the spaces are somewhat different. As it was a well-to-do district, the houses are larger and also more secluded. What is lost in penetrability, however, is gained in movement up and down. In the Small Town many of the secondary streets have steps, and the broken surface relief creates an exceptionally varied richness of urban spaces, which offer ever new perspectives and bits of panoramic views.

The spatial structure of Prague is gathered and condensed in the interiors of its main public buildings. From the

146. St. Nicholas in the Small Town, detail.

Middle Ages on, the local architecture has had its particular spatial properties. In general we note a strong wish for integration and dynamism. The classical principle of individual, static units, which are added together, is unknown in Prague. In St. Vitus the integration, horizontally and vertically, is stronger than in any other great Gothic cathedral, and in the Vladislav Hall (B. Ried 1493-1502) it has become impossible to talk about "bays"; the space is an indivisible whole which is saturated with dynamic movement[7]. The wish for spatial integration and dynamism culminated with the "pulsating" interiors of Christoph and Kilian Ignaz Dientzenhofer[8]. The nave of St. Nicholas in the Small Town by the former (1703-11) consists of a series of interpenetrating ovals. In the vault however, the spatial definition is dislocated relative to the floor. As a result a spatial "syncopation" is created, which represents a unique invention in the history of architecture.

The environmental richness of Prague is intimately related to the spatial properties outlined above. These properties are not only distinguished by variety, but they also constitute an imageable whole. Summing up we may take a look at the basic structure of the four primary domains. The Old Town is situated *on* the flat promontory embraced by the river, and is gathered *around* the Old Town Square. The New Town *fans out* from the Old Town and rises slightly. It is located *between* the St. Vitus hill in the north and the Vyšehrad in the south, and is given internal structure by the three radial markets. Ideally the New Town is a segment of a ring, but the shape is stretched to reach the more distant Vyšehrad. The Small Town is situated *under* the hill, *within* the concave valley, and is gathered *along* the Mostecká-Nerudová path. The Hradčany is *above* the other domains on

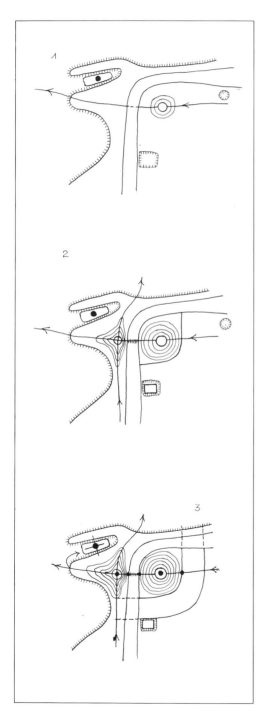

the convex hill, and *stretches out* along a ridge. Whereas the New Town is subordinate to the Old Town and does not possess an independent focus, the other three domains are centred on significant inner cores which have their spatial identity at the same time as they are identified in the townscape by vertical "landmarks". All the domains are integrated by the Charles Bridge. The many prepositions needed to describe the spatial structure of Prague indicate its richness. In general it is *topological* and therefore does not make one particular environmental system manifest. It is open to many interpretations, and teaches us that "orientation" does not only mean imageability, but also "discovery" and "surprise". Knowing Prague is like listening to a great work of music: it always discloses new aspects of itself.

3. Character

The character of Prague cannot be understood without taking the natural environment into consideration. With "natural environment" we do not only have in mind the site of the city, but Bohemia as a whole. For centuries Bohemia has been the object of an exceptionally strong patriotism and love. Not only the historical circumstances have demanded full human identification, but the country as such has given the "Bohemian" a particular identity. In the past this identity was not the property of a single ethnic group. During the religious wars Czech and German speaking people fought together on both sides and the "nation" was first of all a qualitative geographical concept. We may very well say that the inhabitants of Bohemia loved the *genius loci*; the country was theirs because they identified with its qualities. Their love has been expressed in literature and music and not least in building. Few

154. Bohemian landscape.
155. Popular Baroque houses in Třebon.

other countries have an architecture wich is more unified and at the same time more varied. The themes are eminently Bohemian, but the variations are legion and give testimony to the exceptional artistic abilities of the Bohemian people. Like some other great cities, such as Rome, Prague has shaped the foreign artists who have settled there. From Peter Parler to Christoph Dientzenhofer they all became Bohemian and adapted their own cultural import to the local idiom.

What then are the natural phenomena behind the *genius loci*? We have already mentioned the rolling countryside of Bohemia, and the many surprises which break the general continuity of the land. Towards the border these surprises become dominant; wild rocks, hot springs, deep valleys and impenetrable forests bring the original forces of nature into presence. The Bohemian landscape, however, is not characterized by simple imageable elements, such as well defined valley-spaces or dominant mountains. Rather one might say that everything is simultaneously there, a fact which was noticed by Goethe: "Beautiful view over Bohemian landscapes, which have the particular character that they are neither mountains nor plains nor valleys, but everything at the same time"[9]. Obviously the whole of Bohemia does not have this "synthetic" quality. It is, however, the distinctive mark of the more characteristic parts of the country, and therefore becomes a general "Bohemian" trait. Such a generalization is natural, because Bohemia is a simple hydro-geophysical unit.

In Bohemia all the basic natural elements are present within a relatively small and well-defined area. Mountains, vegetation and water are there, not as separate "things", but mixed to form a "romantic" microcosmos. The earth in its different manifestations is exper-

156. *The Small Old Town Square.*
157. *House in the Small Town.*
158. *Palace in the Old Town by K.I.
Dientzenhofer.*

ienced as the primary reality, and asks man for identification. The Bohemian microcosmos is centred on Prague. Not only is Prague situated in the middle, on the river Vltava which in popular imagination is the main identifying element of the country, but its site comprises all the main natural "forces". In Prague we find the juxtaposition of an undulating plain, rocky hills and water. Thus the site beautifully gathers and represents the surrounding country. To experience Prague fully, one therefore has to know Bohemia. It cannot be understood in isolation, but only as a "world within a world".

The same holds true for the architecture of Prague. Although the city was a meeting-place for a multitude of artistic currents, the basic architectural themes are intimately related to the vernacular buildings and settlements of Bohemia. The types of urban spaces are similar; everywhere in the country we find the same continuous but varied streets lined with narrow houses, and the same "ring"-shaped arcaded squares. As typical examples we may mention Ceské Budějovice in the south, Domažlice in the west, Jičin in the north and Litomyšl in the east[10]. The basic settlement pattern is evidently the Slavic ring-village where the "ring" may be round or square. There are in fact towns in Bohemia which only consist of a single row of houses around the square (Nové Město nad Metuji). In some places the houses are small and simple, in others richer, but the basic type is the same. Normally it is a two-storey structure with a third floor in the gable. Arcades are normal when the houses face the square. This may even be the case in small villages with timber houses. The houses have a very particular character, which mainly consists in a massive and heavy appearance. The ground-floor is set directly on the ground, the windows

are low and relatively small, and the wall is usually kept down by the optical weight of large roofs. As a contrast to these ground-hugging properties, richly articulate and ornate gables rise up towards the sky. The houses may have Gothic, Renaissance or Baroque forms, but their basic relationship to earth and sky has remained the same for centuries. Regional differences exist; in Southern Bohemia for instance, the mural houses are white and the decoration richer, but the basic Bohemian qualities are maintained.

In the architecture of Prague the Bohemian relationship to earth and sky reaches a splendid climax. Everywhere the old urban spaces make the basic themes clearly manifest, and the presence of great architects has made possible particular interpretations which make them shine in "limpid brightness". One of the best examples is offered by the house Kilian Ignaz Dientzenhofer built for himself (1726-28) in the suburb of Smichov[11], today known as the *Portheimka*. The rectangular volume has tower-like elements at the four corners and a convex *ressault* in the centre towards the garden. The scheme is "international" and directly derived from Hildebrandt's Upper Belvedere in Vienna. The articulation, however, is truly local. Over the heavy rusticated basement with its low-set windows, the forms become gradually "free" towards the sky. The main architrave is broken in the centre to give place for a pointed gable, whereas the corner towers rise up through the horizontal members. Small blind dormers are added to give emphasis to the vertical movement, and the top cornice of the towers is bent upwards as a last expression of its aspiring force. At the same time however, the towers are tied to the main volume by the horizontal lines which circumscribe the whole building even at

the break in the Mansard roof. A rather violent but subtle interplay of horizontals and verticals is thus created, an interplay which represents a particularly sophisticated interpretation of the basic Prague theme. Another characteristic property may also be pointed out. In general the surface relief of the façade is slight, and the flatness is accentuated by the windows which flush with the wall. The windows thus reflect the colours of the surrounding vegetation and the sky, and give the whole building a certain immaterial feeling which contrasts with the general voluminous character. In certain points strong plastic accents are added which give emphasis to the ambiguous mass-surface relationship. A similar ambiguity is found everywhere in Prague and creates an urban character which is simultaneously sensually earthbound and "spiritualized". Another main work by Kilian Ignaz Dientzenhofer, the St. Nicholas church in the Old Town (1732-37), gives the same themes a "sacred" and truly grandiose interpretation. Here the towers and the central *ressault* free themselves completely but gradually from a continuous, horizontal base, and rise towards the sky with violent dynamism. Other examples could be added *ad infinitum*, and we may also recall that the main Prague *veduta* gets its singular impact from the same "integrated dichotomy" between horizontal and vertical "forces". Thus the buildings of Prague gather and condense the *genius loci*, and make the city appear as a place which is saturated with locally rooted meaning.

The houses which make up the streets and squares of Prague vary the basic themes, and the urban spaces appear as sets of variations, some of them more modest, some more imaginative and splendid. The greatest set of variations is found in the Old Town Square where arcaded gable houses surround most of

the space. They are not mechanically lined up, but constitute a topological succession which gives variety and life to the enclosed space. The houses are quite narrow and create a dynamic movement full of surprises. The variations reach a climax in the stern Týn Church, which prefigures the basic articulation of St. Nicholas near by. The only old building which because of its size breaks the continuity of the boundary, is the Kinsky Palace (1755-66). Again, however, Kilian Ignaz Dientzenhofer demonstrates his artistic abilities and respect for the *genius loci*.[12]. Instead of centering the building on a dominant gate, he doubled the composition, and used two gabled *ressaults* to break down the large volume so as to suit the general dimensions and rhythm of the urban boundary. A similar adaptation is found already in the Toscana Palace by J. B. Mathey (1689) and the Clam-Gallas Palace by Fischer von Erlach (1715ff).

We have characterized Prague as a world where it is possible to penetrate ever deeper "inside", and, in fact, in the interiors of the main buildings we encounter a character which represents a further condensation of the properties which distinguish the urban space and the city as a whole. This character is determined by a particular articulation, which basically remained the same through several centuries. The first great manifestation is the presbytery of the Cathedral by Peter Parler (1352-85)[13]. In general the scheme follows the disposition of the French cathedrals, but the articulation shows several significant innovations. First of all we notice that the arcade is simplified in such a way that it appears as a continuous wall with cut-out openings. At the same time the triforium and the clerestory are combined to form one large glazed surface. The interior is covered by a net-vault which unifies the space horizontally and

makes it dissolve vertically. The horizontal integration is moreover emphasized by the introduction of small, diagonally placed elements in the triforium and clerestory, which make the bays unite in a continuous undulating movement. The space is characterized by a strong contrast between the "massive" arcade and the de-materialized upper wall and vault, and in general by an expressive interplay of horizontal and vertical "forces". We see thus how a generally valid building-type has been modified to suit the *genius loci*.

The same basic traits find a still more original and mature interpretation in the Vladislav Hall in the Hradčany by Benedikt Ried (1493-1502)[14]. Here the interior consists of an integrated series of baldachins which are closed off laterally by massive walls. Two systems are thus combined: the earth-bound "box" made up by the walls, and the de-materialized "heavenly" net-vault which seems to hover over the space.

The theme of the Vladislav Hall reappears in the most significant Baroque buildings of Prague. The "syncopated" space of St. Nicholas in the Small Town is set-into-work by means of an integrated series of baldachins, and the same solution is used in the church of the Březnov Monastery by Christoph Dientzenhofer (1709-15)[15]. In the latter building curved arches span diagonally across the space from wall-pillars (*Wandpfeiler*) which are set against the neutral surface of the massive outer wall. The basic properties of the Vladislav Hall and the churches of Christoph Dientzenhofer are thus the same, and the intention is obviously to make a particular relationship between earth and sky manifest. The exterior of Březnov is also a typical specimen of Prague architecture; a Ionic Order rises over a continuous base, and a row of

dormers and bulging gables create a serrate silhouette.

The intentions of Christoph Dientzenhofer found their continuation in the works of his son, Kilian Ignaz, who may be considered the Prague architect *par excellence*[16]. His most characteristic church in Prague is St. John on the Rock (1730-39). In no other building is the plastic dynamism and dramatic quality so dear to Bohemia expressed with more ability. The church's position on a rock accentuates the effect, and the stair-case in front enhances the vertical movement of the façade. The plan may be described as a "reduced multilateral system of baldachins". On the longitudinal axis of the central octagon with internally convex sides, transverse ovals are added, creating a "pulsating" spatial organism which is enclosed within the kind of continuous, neutral walls we have encountered in the Vladislav Hall and Břevnov. In St. John, however, the plastic form of the exterior corresponds to the interior organization. The outer walls are "wrapped" around the baldachins, and make the interior present in the urban environment. At the same time the walls seem to give in to the pressure of external "forces". Outside and inside thus interact dynamically, and the church becomes a true gathering focus. The interplay of horizontal and vertical movements is also expressed with unique conviction.

Our discussion of the character of the architecture of Prague has implied that the styles of the various epochs were transformed to fit the *genius loci*. The logical structure of High Gothic architecture was changed by Peter Parler to express the local horizontal-vertical dichotomy. In St. Vitus we cannot any more distinguish the different shafts which "carry" arches and vaults, and in the Old Town bridge-tower by the same Parler (after 1375) the Gothic elements

168. *St. John on the Rock by K.I. Dientzenhofer.*
169. *St. John on the Rock, interior.*
170. *The Czernin Palace by F. Caratti.*
171. *The Belvedere.*

have become a "decoration" applied to a massive volume[17]. The non-structural interpretation of Gothic forms culminated with the Vladislav Hall, where the originally structural ribs have become a dynamic ornament which cannot possibly be subdivided logically into *partes* and *membra*[18]. In Bohemia, thus, Gothic de-materialization is not understood as a "spiritual system" which conquers and substitutes the bodily substance, but as an ecstatic liberation from the earth. "Ecstacy" in fact means "out of place".

During the Renaissance and Baroque we encounter analogous intentions. The classical Orders are there, but they are used in a new way and are partly transformed. A certain anti-classical attitude is already evident in the Belvedere garden-palace, which was started by Italian architects in pure Renaissance forms (1534). Later a swelling concave-convex roof was added (1563) which transforms the building into a plastic volume which is simultaneously earth-bound and aspiring. Another characteristic transformation of Renaissance forms is found in the Czernin Palace by Francesco Caratti (1668ff), where Palladio has become Bohemian! In the buildings of the Dientzenhofers the classical Orders also play a primary role, but not as characterizing elements which give the single work an individual presence; rather they serve to visualize the dynamic vertical forces which saturate the buildings. Similarly the horizontal members are bent, broken or interrupted to express the basic dichotomy which constitutes the essence of the Bohemian character. And the single motifs of classical architecture, such as brackets, pediments and key stones, lose their systematic meaning and become plastic accents which make the continuity of the spatial boundary still more evident. Thus classical architecture is absorbed by a more ancient

world of forces, a mystical world which seizes us with irresistible power.

4. Genius Loci

Our analysis of the spatial structure and character of Prague, has uncovered the basic manifestations of a very strong *genius loci*. Which meanings does this "spirit" gather? We have already described the natural "forces" which constitute its local basis, and understand how Prague first of all is the true and meaningful focus of a delimited and characteristic region. Its "mystery" is nothing artificial but a reflection of a given natural environment. The "ecstatic" interpretation of this environment, however, also reflects the history of the country. In Bohemia it has always been necessary to *fight* for an existential foothold, and the roots had to be very deep to withstand the alien forces which over and over again threatened the local form of life. Deep roots mean intense identification, and under the particular Bohemian circumstances this also implied an intensely felt relationship to the foreign import. The religious conflicts which after the burning of Jan Hus (1369-1415), for over two hundred years determined the political and cultural life of Europe, had their centre of gravity in Bohemia, and in our own time Czechoslovakia has again been a prey of various forces.

In addition to its local qualities, the *genius loci* of Bohemia also reflects many "influences". The Slavic background of the Czech people is clearly evident, and forms of eastern origin are often encountered; we may mention in particular the small onion-shaped domes on towers and steeples, as well as a love for silhouettes which remind of Russian churches and monasteries. Still stronger is the German influence, but the imported themes, such as the *Hallenkirche* and the *Wandpfeilerkirche*, became thoroughly transformed when they were planted in the Bohemian soil. The Bohemian Renaissance and Baroque are unthinkable without Italian import; in particular does the local Baroque represent the most fertile development of the ideas of Borromini and Guarini[19]. Even French currents reached Bohemia, both through Austria and directly from the French architect Jean-Baptiste Mathey who worked in Prague for over twenty years. In all these cases, however, the foreign import was transformed by the genius loci. As a result a very comprehensive synthesis was formed, where fragments of various derivation appear as "memories" which intermingle like *tesserae* in a truly cosmopolitan mosaic.

In general the Bohemian synthesis was felt as a dichotomy between body and spirit. One has talked about the motherly warm and simultaneously ecstatic character of Bohemian religiosity[20], but warmth and ecstasy do not always work together. In the Italian *cinquecento*, the relationship between body and spirit was felt as a problematic split, which in the work of Michelangelo was expressed as a fundamental human problem. A solution was offered by Baroque art, where ecstatic participation brought about a sense of meaning and security. Also in Bohemia the Baroque offered a solution to the local situation, and we understand why the Baroque became the Bohemian art *par excellence*. But participation is open to various interpretations. In the work of the Dientzenhofers it was a means of redemption; their baldachin-structures bring heaven close at the same time as the earth is approached with confidence and love. The latter aspect is concretized by the simultaneously open and substantial walls which are wrapped around the baldachins. Another architect of the eighteenth century however, Johann Santin Aichel[21] gave Bohemian architecture a different interpretation. In his works heaven remains distant and inaccessible, at the same time as the space is enclosed by walls of a "cold" and somewhat frightening character. His particular use of abstract "Gothic" forms moreover deprives the buildings of any anthropomorphous warmth. Instead of the assurance of the Dientzenhofers we experience a tragic world where human imprisonment seems an eternal condition. The work of Santin Aichel is not an isolated phenomenon; in the writings of Kafka a similar interpretation reappears with intense actuality, and in Bohemian art in general up to present day Czech surrealism, the "tragic" view is always there as a meaningful undercurrent[22].

Regardless of interpretation, however, Bohemian architecture has conserved its particular identity, and Prague its role as the place where the character is condensed and explained. Out in the country we encounter the Bohemian themes in somewhat crude form; exceptionally heavy and massive houses and castles, slender steeples crowned by onion-shaped domes, a picturesque and varied use of colour. In Prague this elements are gathered and unified; what is primarily local becomes universal, and what is foreign is adapted to the place. But gathering also means feed-back, it means that the "explanation" given at the centre radiates back so that the provinces may gain a full understanding of their role within the totality. Hardly any city has ever fulfilled this role more convincingly than *Praga caput regni*.

The structure of the *genius loci* of Prague is also confirmed by the fact that the city has conserved so well its identity throughout the course of history. The basic spatial structure was suggested by the natural place and fixed from the very beginning. The successive rulers of

Prague have not attempted the introduction of any abstract or foreign scheme, but adapted their contributions to what was there before. The Baroque, for instance, did not change the urban structure, but gave emphasis to the old foci by means of new buildings such as the two St. Nicholas churches by the Dientzenhofers. It furthermore gave the old houses new façades without changing the environmental character. A similar conservation of the *genius loci* is also found in other Czechoslovak cities, such as Telč, where Mediaeval, Renaissance, and Baroque houses line up along the grandiose market as members of one large family. The fascination of Prague to a high extent depends on its extraordinary continuity; it is as if a powerfull will has demanded the cooperation of ever. new generations to create a unique work of urban art.

Today Prague is different and still the same. The cosmopolitan community is gone and the colourful popular life of the past has disappeared. The economic structure has also undergone profound changes, and the old city of merchants has had to accomodate new functions and institutions. But the place is still there with its urban spaces and its character, beautifully restored with its Late Baroque polychromy, allowing for an orientation and identification which goes beyond the security or threat offered by the immediate economic or political system. From the new residential neighborhoods people go to old Prague to get a confirmation of their identity. Without the old centre, Prague would today be sterile and the inhabitants would be reduced to alienated ghosts. After the old Ghetto had been torn down around 1900, Kafka said: "They are still alive in us, the dark corners, the mysterious alleys, blind windows, dirty courtyards, noisy taverns and secretive inns. We walk about the

broad streets of the new town, but our steps and looks are uncertain. We tremble inwardly as we used to do in the old miserable lanes. Our hearts know nothing yet of any clearance. The unsanitary old ghetto is much more real to us than our new, hygienic surroundings. We walk about as in a dream, and are ourselves only a ghost of past times"[23].

1. *Image*

Those who visit Khartoum are immediately struck by a strong *quality of place*. The horizontal expanse of the barren desert country, the slow movement of the great life-giving Nile, the immense sky and the burning sun, combine to create a singularly powerful environment.

Many places along the Nile obviously have similar properties, but at Khartoum the situation is particular: here the two Niles meet, the majestic white river from the South and the swifter blue current from the East.

We feel that we are no longer just somewhere in the longitudinal oasis created by the Nile, but at a "crossroad", a meeting-place which invites men to come together and dwell. And the bustling, colourful life of the city confirms our spontaneous interpretation of the natural situation.

The quality of Khartoum as a place is not only determined by geography and landscape. Although the city does not possess any heritage of great architectural monuments, the urban environment has structure as well as distinct character. First of all the visitor spontaneously perceives the three settlements which make up Khartoum, as different but interrelated places. In fact Khartoum is generally known as the "Three Towns". The wide regular streets of the colonial city which were planned by lord Kitchener after the British conquest in 1898, form a meaningful counterpoint to the labyrinthine world of Arabic Omdurman which was the capital of Sudan during the Mahdist regime (1885-98). Khartoum North, finally, combines both characters, and relates them to the world of a present-day industrial town. As a fourth, profoundly significant element we find the landscape and vernacular settlement of Tuti island, which gives the visitor a sense of

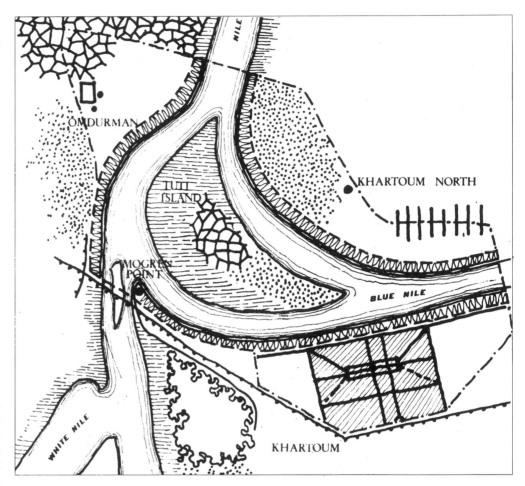

180. *Old houses in Omdurman.*
181. *The suk in Khartoum.*
182. *The building of a mud house within the perimeter wall.*

elementary rootedness. This settlement is the oldest in the conurbation dating from the 1560'ies. Being situated where the two Niles meet, Tuti forms the real core or "heart" of Khartoum. This core, however, is not a monumental urban centre, but a manifestation of a simple, archetypal relationship between man and nature, which, as one gets to know the place better, becomes deeply meaningful.

Our experience of Khartoum is also determined by its vast dimensions. The Niles are very wide, and as the three towns are somewhat withdrawn from their banks, a unified visual image becomes impossible. The different districts within the conurbation are thus experienced as being *distant* from each other. Khartoum, in fact, is not a city where you can take a walk to get acquainted with the place! We may say that its scale is in tune with the surrounding country and even with its position on the African continent. And still Khartoum possesses that intimacy which is a distinctive property of any true place. The streets of colonial Khartoum are accompanied by arcades and trees which give us spatial foothold, the narrow lanes and courtyards of Omdurman are true "interior worlds", and in both towns the *suk*, or market, is a focus for social life where the individual may experience participation and belonging. Here we touch upon the essence of Khartoum's quality of place: the combination of grand external relations and true interiority.

The external relations of Khartoum however, are not the usual networks of roads and railways. Not a single road connects the metropolis with the rest of the world! To arrive in Khartoum one has to drive through the surrounding desert. In the desert no direction is of primary importance and a feeling of general openness results. This physical

isolation implies that the figural character of the place is emphasized: Khartoum thus possesses the ancient quality of appearing as a "figure" on a continuous natural background, which here is uniform and without prominent topographical features. Everywhere the desert is present; not only at the periphery of the habitat it enters between the houses, but also at the very centres of the three towns we have the sand of the desert under our feet, and everywhere we feel its infinite expanse. Even in the wooded areas close to the river, such as the attractive Sunt Forest between Khartoum proper and the right bank of the White Nile, the trees grow as "individuals" on a continuous surface of sand. During the frequent sand storms the desert becomes a threatening existential fact.

The only element which is strong enough to oppose the desert is the Nile. But the river does not bring any drama into the general calm of the natural environment. Neither it creates any enclosed valley space within the flat, extended land[1]. The simple unity of natural space is emphasized by the immense, cloudless sky, and the intense sunlight which penetrates everywhere and makes any distinction between *natural* "exteriors" and "interiors" meaningless. It is a kind of *pitiless* world, which although it offers man life, leaves it to him alone to create a space where he can dwell and develop the values of community and privacy.

In spite of their diversity the Three Towns have one basic fact in common: they allow for dwelling in a desert country. Primarily this is schieved by *enclosing an area* by means of a fence or a wall. Traditionally, the walls were made of mud or sun-dried brick, a technique which is still commonly used, and which gives large parts of the Three Towns a uniform character. The *houses*

184. *Diagrammatic map of the Niles.*
185. *The watersheds of Africa.*
186. *The local settlement pattern between desert and longitudinal oasis.*
187. *The desert at Khartoum.*

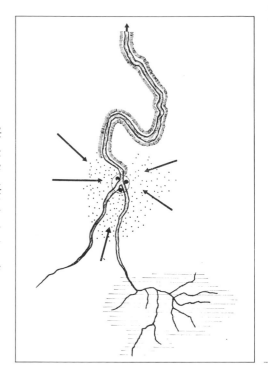

are also built of mud and brick, and their totally closed, prismatic shape represents a clear response to the challenge of the desert. Whereas the desert is what man has to escape from, and accordingly was related by the ancient Egyptians to Death, the house is a protected world where Life may blossom. It is not surprising, hence, that the transition between these two realms becomes an important, "architectural" problem. In Khartoum, the entrance is something more than a passage from the public to the private domain. On the richly decorated gates the colours of the interior appear, to tell about a friendlier world created by man, where the fresh character of white, light green and blue substitutes the burning yellow and brown of the exterior world. The settlement pattern which better answers the challenge of the desert, is the dense labyrinth, and all the old villages found within the Khartoum conurbation as well as the town of Omdurman, belong to this archetype. Colonial Khartoum however possesses a different urban structure. And still it does not feel foreign to the place.

We shall return to this problem later. So far we only want to point out that the Three Towns plus the villages represent different interpretations of the same *genius loci*.

2. Space

An area of vast extension gravitates on Khartoum. Whereas European centres as a rule are related to defined regions of a limited size, Khartoum is "surrounded" by "infinite" expanses of scarcely populated desert and savannah. The only prominent structural element is the Nile, which for thousands of kilometres cuts through the country from the south to the north. Had it not been for the river, the entire area would have appeared quite inarticulate as a geographical en-

tity. The Nile valley proper, however, which determines the character of Egypt, only starts further north. At Khartoum the land is flat, and is *open* to the surrounding regions, rather then possessing the absolute self-sufficiency of the Egyptian Nile valley, or the forbidding indeterminateness of the Sudd swamps further to the south. This open land lacks any true "microstructure". Only a few shallow *wadis* break the monotonous extension of the ground. Natural places are therefore rare. Because of the confluence of the two Niles, however, the expanse of the desert is divided into three domains, among which *El Gezira* (i.e. "the peninsula") between the two rivers is particularly distinct.

The meeting of geographical regions is accompanied by corresponding climatic, ethnic and cultural relationships. At Khartoum the rainless desert of North Africa approaches the humid belt which crosses the continent at both sides of the Equator. Accordingly, vegetation starts to make itself felt, at the same time as the desert remains a fundamental environmental force. The great Arabic-Islamic desert culture is therefore the primary existential fact. In the Sudan however, the pure and abstract absolutism of Islam meets the magic world of Africa proper. Khartoum is thus at the centre of several "worlds": the "eternal" order of the Nile valley to the North, the world of black Africa to the South, the infinite desert to the West, and the harsh mountains of Etiopia further away to the East. A map of the watersheds of Africa moreover shows Sudan as an "interior space" of singular importance, as the other African regions are related to a coast. The *situation* of Khartoum thus offers man excellent possibilities of orientation: here he is not just somewhere in Africa, but in one of the places from which geography may

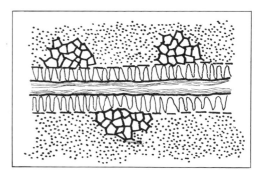

be understood as a meaningful system of spatial relationships.

How then does the *site* satisfy this spatial role? Evidently the openess of the landscape is favourable, as it does not put any narrow limits to the place, at the same time as the confluence of the Niles fulfills the basic need for place-definition. The division of the zone in three domains has already been mentioned as a main structural feature. The "longitudinal oasis" along the rivers, finally, makes the place particularly suited for settlement. The natural landscape therefore has a spatial structure which gathers and expresses the geographical relationships. It would be tempting to mention Tuti island in this connection, as it is located at the very centre of the site. Being an island, however, Tuti does not possess those external relations which form an important part of the meaning of the Khartoum conurbation as a capital centre. Therefore it has been left in its original state as a limited, fertile world within the "vast unknown" of the desert. Rather than being the real focus, Tuti illustrates the original settlement pattern of the region. Here we may still experience that "living cell" which forms the basis for dwelling in the desert. Because Tuti is left out of the development of the capital as an urban "pause", the confluence point of the two Niles, Moqren, assumes the role of a main focal point.

The original settlement pattern found at Tuti, is also preserved in some villages within the area of the conurbation. If we take a look at the old agricultural settlements which are today incorporated in the urban texture of the Three Towns (Halfaya, Abu Said, Hamad, Khogali etc.), we find that they are not located on the river, but *between* the river oasis and the desert. They are with-drawn from the Nile, and are thus very different from European river settlements. Basically they are *desert* villages, and the desert is experienced as omnipresent. The practical reasons obviously are to preserve agricultural land as to get away from areas of seasonal inundation. But the location of the villages also expresses the necessity of living *with* the desert, rather than behaving as if it were not there.

The Three Towns preserve this archetypal pattern. Even in Colonial Khartoum we find that the urban streets are separated from the Nile by a continuous green belt, and in all three towns the urban centres have hardly any contact with the river. In general we may conclude that the basic settlement pattern of Khartoum is meaningful, and expresses a deep "understanding" of the natural situation. The life-giving role of the Nile only becomes manifest if its banks are left as continuous green belts, and the great existential fact of the desert ought to be felt everywhere within the habitat.

This does not mean, however, that the settlements should spread out. A desert village or town ought to be dense; that is, it should be something we *enter*, a place we are *within*, to find a foothold in the infinite expanse of the surrounding country. But it would be wrong to interpret this density as a cluster of highrise buildings.

The main existential dimension of the desert is the *horizontal*, and the Arabs in fact have always preferred low, horizontally extended buildings (except in mountainous countries such as Yemen or Marocco).

The only vertical element is the slender needle of the Minaret, which reminds man that he does not only live on earth but also under the sky. The old villages as well as the town of Omdurman illustrate this principle of "dense horizontality".

Colonial Khartoum also shows a coherent, horizontal development, and although its geometrical plan was imported, the town in general demonstrates a satisfactory understanding of the site. The embankment along the Blue Nile, where North and South meet, is thus treated as a continuous green belt, but rather than being a piece of nature, it is interpreted as a "balcony" from which the role of Khartoum as a centre may be experienced. The incorporation of the cardinal points in the plan moreover expresses the geographic situation outlined above.

The three domains formed by the confluence of the Niles are symbolized by the Three Towns, and the three-polar structure of the conurbation thus represents a further concretization of the geographic situation. Moreover their spatial patterns are in accordance with the different role of the domains within the totality. This fact is proved by the alternation between Khartoum and Omdurman as the capital of Sudan. Whereas Omdurman is the "spearhead" of an Arabic hinterland, Khartoum assumes a more cosmopolitan function. Today the Three Towns are linked to form a "ring-structure", which well expresses the new historical situation.

Two basic types of urban structure are found in the Three Towns: the labyrinthine world of the desert settlement, and a geometrical pattern of "Baroque" derivation which symbolizes a general ideological system. Of these, the labyrinthine pattern represents the original, vernacular solution. In fact, it is especially dense at Tuti, where the island site adds a particular "intimacy" to the general interiority of the labyrinth. The lanes at Tuti are very narrow, and continuously changing their direction. Variations in width, and breaks in the space-defining walls do away with the rests of simple, Euclidean order. As a

188. *The Blue Nile at Khartoum with longitudinal oasis.*
189. *Extended horizontal houses at the periphery of Khartoum.*

result, the feeling of elementary togetherness is very strong. In Khogali the openness of the descrt is more felt; the cluster stretches out and the streets widen somewhat. The same is the case in old Omdurman (such as the Abu Rouf and Beit El Mal districts), where a certain change in scale is also apparent, indicating the historically more important role of the town. But the basic interiority of the Arabic settlement is still preserved. The labyrinthine parts of the Three Towns were generated by a gradual clustering of units, leaving the streets as secondary "intervals". This approach to urban "design" is still used in the squatter settlements along the periphery, which thus repeat the constituent principle of Arabic towns. The spaces formed in this way have an eminently human quality, changing shape and size according to the needs. Only in the new city-extensions north of Omdurman and south of Khartoum, carried out after the second world war according to a master-plan by Doxiadis, the *street* is taken as the point of departure, whereby the urban spaces lose their traditional quality.

In Colonial Khartoum the circulation infrastructure is the primary fact, but in contrast to the undetermined grid of Doxiadis, if forms a sophisticated symbolic pattern which takes general as well as local factors into consideration. It is probably true that Kitchener used the "Union Jack" as his model when he planned the orthogonal and diagonal streets of Khartoum. But the pattern fortunately has a meaning which goes beyond this "imperialistic" content. As a "cosmic" symbol it also represents the general natural order of the cardinal points. Throughout history the orthogonal axes were used to express any absolute system, often in combination with a pronounced centre. In this sense they were also employed in the early

191. *Urban structure (Khogali).*

192. *The Khogali district of North Khartoum.*
193. *Squatter settlement.*
194. *Street from the Doxiadis extension.*

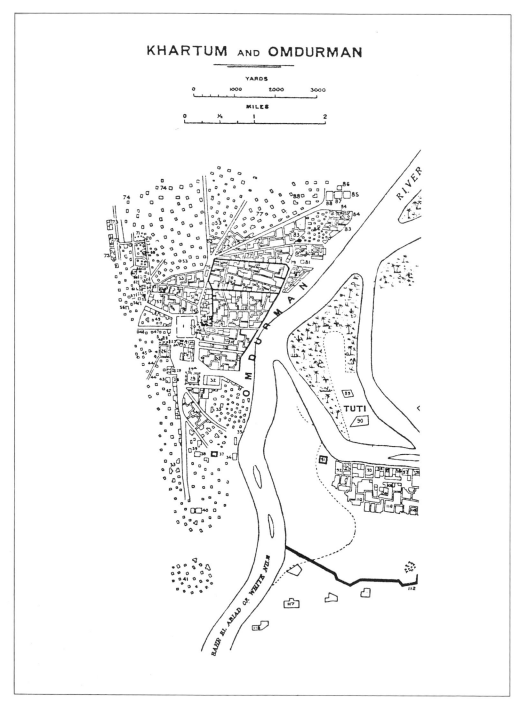

195. *Old map of Khartoum and Omdurman showing Khartoum before the destruction.*

KHARTUM AND OMDURMAN

YARDS

0   1000   2000   3000

MILES

0   ½   1   2

Islamic capital of Baghdad. In European Baroque architecture diagonal axes were introduced to express the "openness" of the system. No wonder, hence, that the same pattern was adopted for the colonial capital of Khartoum. In addition to these general properties, Kitchener's solution shows some particular traits which ought to receive due attention. If we take a look at the town plan, we notice an interesting doubling of the main North-South axis. Parallel to El Qasr Avenue (formerly Victoria Avenue) which runs between the War Memorial (Railway Station, Faculty of Medicine) and the Palace, we thus find another equally important street, El Khalifa-El Gami Avenue, which has the great Mosque at its centre. This street divides the main square in two equal halves, and is moreover symmetrically related to the pattern of diagonal streets. The plan from 1904 proves that this state of affairs is the original one. Thus it is El Khalifa-El Gami Avenue and not El Qasr, which geometrically forms the main axis of the urban network, and it is the *Mosque* which is found at the very centre of the system. Its *qibla*-orientation at 45° to the main axes moreover makes it parallel to the diagonals of the "Union Jack". The directions of the plan are thus just as Islamic as they are Britannic! On this pattern, the wide, dominant El Qasr Avenue and the Palace are superimposed as a "foreign", albeit centrally located, counterpoint. Certainly an interesting and meaningful urban structure.

The streets and squares of Colonial Khartoum form a continuous, differentiated public domain. We have already mentioned the primary function of some of the avenues, and should add that the main east-west street, El Gamhuriya Avenue (formerly Sirdar Avenue) serves as the centre's commercial spine. Between the green belt along the Nile

196. *Lord Kitchener's plan for Khartoum.*
197. *The Great Mosque of Khartoum.*
198. *Colonial Khartoum, El Khalifa-El Gami Avenue.*

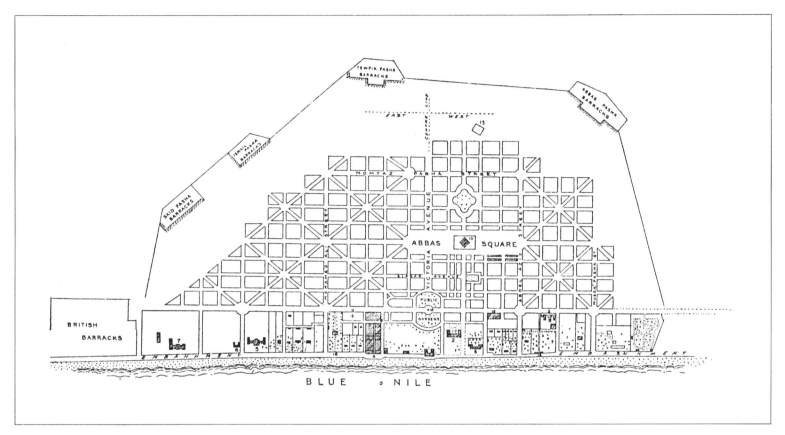

199. *Corner kiosk.*
200. *Residential street in Omdurman.*

and the built town another main axis, El Gamia Avenue, is running east-west. As it gives access to principal public buildings such as churches, ministeries and University (formerly Gordon College) which are located within the green belt itself, it had from the beginning a representative function. Interpolated between the main urban corridors, we find a secondary network of service alleys. The system is surpisingly modern, and corresponds to the movement structure advocated in recent traffic-in-town planning theory. In this system the squares do not serve as real "goals", but rather as nodal points. The system therefore never comes to any conclusion, but remains "open", and was in fact extended and modified several times[2]. Within the public network of Colonial Khartoum, private spaces are "filled in" with a certain degree of freedom. The typical dwelling unit is a suburban villa of European derivation, which is adapted to local conditions by the introduction of perimeter walls and garden porticoes. Continuous porticoes also accompany the commercial streets, distinguishing them spatially from the streets of the residential zones which are usually defined by closed walls or garden fences. Often the corners of the blocks are emphasized functionally and spatially by arcades kiosks, a motif which is evidently taken over from a local tradition; such kiosks are even found at Tuti island.

In the vernacular parts of the conurbation we encounter a more genuine type of private space. Here the enclosed area is the basic unit, and the perimeter wall with an ornate gate is traditionally built before the dwelling itself. Within the enclosed area there are usually several one-room houses, free-standing or attached to the perimeter. The houses divide the area into one part for men, which is located immediately behind the gateway and has a certain representative function, and another, more withdrawn, for women, children and domestic functions in general. The rooms are treated as enclosed secondary spaces within the main space; the windows are small and their wooden shutters rarely open. Sitting furniture (chairs, sofas) is disposed along the perimeter, creating thus a centralized order. Large niches or columned porticoes may form a transition between the courtyards and the rooms. In general the Khartoum house reflects the traditional interiority and subdivision of the Arabic dwelling, but the disposition is less formal (urban) than in the typical North-African *dar*, where the courtyard tends to be a regular square centred on a fountain.

Our discussion of the settlement pattern and urban structure has shown that the Khartoum conurbation has a imageable and meaningful spatial organization. The very simple spatial elements offered by nature, are taken as the point of departure for a man-made environment, which facilitates orientation and image-making. As a totality the confluence of the Niles and the Three Towns form a very "strong" Gestalt, and the different urban structures of Omdurman and Colonial Khartoum create a meaningful complexity within the totality. The image of Omdurman may be described as a "textural domain" or cluster, centred on a double node formed by the Mahdi Square and the *suk*. Khartoum is a geometrical network, within which landmarks and nodes are distributed according to their functional and symbolic role. Khartoum North is less distinct, but possesses an impressive landmark in the Khogali mosque and tomb. The Three Towns are united by the blue-green belt of the Nile, which appears as a natural figure on a desert ground.

125

3. Character

The natural character of Khartoum is determined by the concrete appearance of the site. Undoubtedly the most prominent element is the *sand* of the desert. The inhabitants of the Three Towns are so to speak born from sand; they have sand under their feet the whole life, and are buried in sand when they die. And sand is omnipresent, not only as a material, but as colour and texture. Its fine grain seems to express the effect of the buring sun on the more solid materials which make up our earth, and make us again remember the ancient Egyptians who built artificial mountains, pyramids, to withstand the destructive forces of the desert. Sand is thus the unifying ground of this world, and its golden-brown-grey colour relates the same world to materials as different as precious gold and dirty mud. In the short rainy season, in fact, the ground is transformed into a continuous mire, whereas the setting sun makes the same surface become a golden field. The predominance of sand gives the landscape a barren character. But it is not the barrenness of rocky and mountainous regions where the varied topography still gives nourishment to man's imagination. A flat surface of sand, instead, does not offer many possibilities of identification, it is indeed something man deserts. When this is practically not possible, man has to add something himself, which allows for identification with a wider range of existential meanings.

In Khartoum, however, nature itself offers something more. The reliable Nile makes it possible to endure the desert, and the oasis along its banks gives a promise of life. An oasis, however, is not something alien to the desert. Rather the oasis *grows out of* the desert, it "dwells" *in* the desert. The palm tree expresses this relationship particularly

126

204. *The desert.*
205. *The Nile at Gordon's Trih.*

well, appearing suddenly out of the sandy ground which is left as such, and rising high before it unfolds in a crown of large leaves. The palm tree therefore does not create any microstructure, it does not define spaces within space, but only represents an invitation for settling. It offers man friendship rather than a house. But the tall, slender trunks introduce a rhythm in the monotonous expanse of the desert. Obviously the trees are not growing at equal intervals, but their simple form and relatively unifom size create an impression of spatial regularity. The palm grove is probably one of the archetypal images which have determined the lay-out of the early Umayyad mosques, with their "forest" of columns. If this is true, it implies that the palm grove was understood as a sacred place where the life-giving forces become manifest within the "dead" desert.

Water is not enough to produce a manifestation of life. The life-giving force *par excellence* is light. Here in the middle of Africa, the intensity of the sun is still stronger than even in Egypt. In fact it becomes a threat to life[3]. Man cannot live without the sun, but here he also has to ask for protection against its terrible radiation and heat. The light is without nuances; with full intensity it fills space under a cloudless sky. No subtle transitions lead from light to shadow. Either you close the sun out, or you are exposed to its full impact. The light of Khartoum therefore has a place-consuming rather than a place-creating function, and completes that natural world which we have already characterized as "pitiless". Here dwelling becomes a problem which asks for elementary and strong interventions, and architecture is "reduced" to true essentials.

Nor wonder, hence, that the architecture of Khartoum has a distinct and

206. *Palm trees in front of Khartoum Palace.*
207. *Old Omdurman.*
208. *Vernacular architecture at its best.*

209. *Old mud architecture.*
210. *Old house in Omdurman, courtyard.*

uniform character. Experiments and personal idiosyncracies are meaningless in this world; if you do not obey to the "laws" of the natural environment, life becomes impossible. The dependence of man upon nature is first of all expressed through the use of local materials and colours. The vernacular houses of the Three Towns are made of mud or sun-dried brick, and also the burnt brick traditionally employed in more important public structures, adapt the buildings to the character of the given environment. The perimeter wall which is the primary element of the dwelling, appears as a continuous, enclosing surface. Windows are few and small, and in older houses they have a round form which characterize them as *holes* in a closed wall. Corners and cornices are also round, and thereby emphasize the massive character. At the same time the wall gets a hand-made, humanized appearance. The only element which breaks the somewhat monotonous course of the residential lanes and streets, arc the beforementioned gateways, which signal the private world behind the walls. (A richly ornate gateway is also a status symbol). The pronounced enclosure of the private domain is in accordance with the social structure of the Arabs, which, on the other hand, also developed through an interaction between man and a particular natural environment[4].

Nature, dwelling and social structure are hence interdependent aspects of one organic totality. The plastic modelling and "soft" details, however, are African rather than Arabic. The Arabic architecture of North Africa in fact gives more emphasis to regularity and geometrization[5]. The vernacular architecture of Khartoum thus represents an interesting synthesis of Arabic and African characters.

When we enter the interior of the

dwelling, that is, the private domain proper, we encounter a new environmental character.

Here the desert is no longer the dominant force; the wall has closed it out, and the green of vegetation and blue of water substitute the sun and sand colours of exterior space.

Traditionally plants and water ought to be present, and in addition partitions and other architectural elements are painted in the same refreshing colours. The glazed tiles used in Arabic countries are however lacking; the architecture of Khartoum is less sophisticated. But the basic character is the same; a character which stems from the need to create an "inside" where life is protected physically and psychologically against the pitiless world outside. In a desert country it is necessarily imagined as an isolated, artificial garden, where those meanings which cannot prosper outside are concretized. This "inside" may be likened to a living cell. As such it cannot grow and conquer the hostile environment, but more cells may be added until a true organism results. We understand, thus, that the characteristic type of additive settlement pattern described above, stems from the concretization of a particular environmental character. Even in the simplest Islamic dwelling this is the case, such as the Bedouin tent, where the bright colours of the blankets and the centralized disposition of the beds and the hearth make a similar interiority manifest.

When several private compounds are added up, a public domain is created. This domain consists of several components: the semi-private access street, the public corridor street, and the eminently public *suk*, where the profane functions of social life are focused. In Omdurman and the vernacular villages of the conurbation, the characteristic Islamic blind alley is relatively rare, but

130

212. *Colonial house in Khartoum with Ionic columns.*
213. *The Khartoum suk with arcades.*
214. *Arcades in Colonial Khartoum.*

the residential streets anyhow have the private and somewhat forbidding character known from other Islamic towns. The private character is obviously determined by the densely spaced, closed perimeter walls of the dwellings. In Colonial Khartoum, instead, the houses are open to the environment: continuous porticoes run along their fronts, and the enclosing wall is often substituted by a transparent fence. A Nordic wish for "contact with nature" is echoed by these forms. The very substance of the buildings is also changed: instead of amorphous, "topological" walls we find columns, arches and architraves; that is, the anthropomorphous elements of classical European architecture. The columns are throughout Ionic; prefabricated of concrete! The classical members as well as the open porticoes, give the colonial houses a semi-public appearance, a character which was not quite out of place, considering that they were built for the people who ruled the country. Even today the houses are inhabited by government officials and diplomats!

Similar porticoes were used to characterize the public buildings of Colonial Khartoum; in smaller buildings prefabricated Ionic columns were also employed, whereas the main structures show specially designed, monumental versions of the portico theme. In the commercial streets and market areas the porticoes join to form continuous arcades. As a result, urban space interacts with the volume of the building, expressing its public character. An *urban* "inside" is thus created, which is enhanced by the introduction of trees. Kitchener, in fact, had 7,000 trees planted in Colonial Khartoum. Along the Blue Nile embankment they create a kind of "natural portico" which forms a beautiful transition between the built town and the river landscape. The

215. *The Khartoum embankment seen from Tuti.*
216. *The Khartoum (Blue Nile) embankment.*
217. *The Khartoum embankment.*
218. *The Omdurman suk, typical alley.*
219. *The Omdurman suk, main street.*

urban spaces of Colonial Khartoum therefore do not follow the Islamic principles of city building. In the Islamic city porticoes are usually employed around enclosed courtyards; together with trees and water they belong to that interior world described above[6]. In accordance with a European concept of the city, Kitchener turned these enclosed "oases" inside out, transforming thus the whole urban milieu into a human alternative to the desert. The solution may seem foreign to the place, and the wide streets of Khartoum may indeed lose their spatial meaning under the impact of the burning sun. They are saved, however, by the arcades and the trees, and thus express a new possible way of dwelling in a desert country[7]. Similar arcades have also been introduced in the main street of Omdurman, which leads up to the *suk* area. In the *suk* itself we experience, instead, the Arabic type of public milieu. Being the largest market on the African continent, it consists of a large number of densely grouped one-story shop compounds, separated by narrow lanes. The interior furnishing of the shops follow the U-pattern already encountered in the Arabic dwelling. Such units add up to form rows which open on the lanes. They are not, however, joined together by common arcades. Rather they maintain a certain independence and flexibility, which is expressed by variations in entrance verandas and roof overhangs. Wood, metal and concrete predominate here, not mud and brick as in the residential areas.

The arcaded porticoes which are a characteristic feature of the public architecture of Khartoum, are distinguished by a rather unusual articulation. Rather than consisting of a regular succession of similar intervals, they create a more complex *rhythm* where wide and narrow intervals alternate. In

220. *Kiosk with rhythmically disposed openings.*
221. *Monumental colonial architecture.*
222. *Lord Kitchener's Palace.*

the corner kiosks this treatment becomes a basic motif: a wide arched opening is flanked by one narrow slot on each side. The shop-front proper (mostly of wood) is usually placed a couple of metres behind the outer wall. In the commercial areas several such facades may be linked together, forming a more or less continuous series of arcades, where the alternation of wide and narrow openings gives the urban space a lively but ordered rhythm.

In most of the public buildings designed for Lord Kitchener, this facade articulation is adopted and varied in a fascinating way. Its recurrence in almost all buildings of importance proves that it has been deliberately intended, and it is moreover varied with much understanding for the building task in question.

In some smaller structures, the typical Ionic columns are simply placed at rhythmical intervals. In a larger building such as the Grand Hotel, the theme is used to form a transition between the wings and the main central *ressault*. In the ministries and the University, rhythmically placed columns are engaged with piers to obtain a "monumental" character. (The University moreover has pointed arches, probably to recall the Gothic colleges in England). In the Palace, finally, the width of the arches becomes a flexible means to define the primary and secondary axes of the grandiose layout. As historical research is lacking, it is not possible to furnish a secure interpretation of the interesting motif. It is certainly not European import, and neither it can be related to the regular repetition of intervals which distinguishes Islamic architecture. It is tempting to understand the solution as an *African* (Egyptian?) trait, which succeeds in giving the imported forms a local stamp.

Buildings having a *sacred* character are

134

relatively rare in the Three Towns. They are mainly of two types: square hall mosques flanked by slender minarets, and domed tombs. The main mosques of Colonial Khartoum and Omdurman are based in the simple grid pattern which distinguishes the sacred spaces of classical Islam. The articulation of the exteriors therefore does not show the rhythmical treatment discussed above. The Mahdi tomb in Omdurman and the Khogali tomb in Khartoum North have steep, pointed domes which may reflect the influence of the circular huts of the region.

Our discussion of the architectural forms and articulation has shown that the Three Towns possess a meaningful universe of characters. The natural environment is simple and strong, and determines the general character of the milieu. This does not mean, however, that it satisfies man's need for identification. Although he has to be a friend of the desert to dwell here, he also has to add an artificial world of his own. That is, he has to withdraw into a psychologically and socially meaningful "interior", from which he may return to the desert as a "conqueror" either through the local adding up of such interiors (dwellings), or through the propagation of their cultural message. The Khartoum conurbation is to a high extent determined by such "messages" from the outside: Islamic, European or African, but they have been adapted to the particular local conditions, to allow for a human identification which is not merely cultural but directly related to the place.

4. *Genius Loci*

The landscape of Khartoum has a pronounced "cosmic" quality. The infinitely extended, roadless desert, the east-west trajectory of the sun, and the south-north axis of the Nile create a

singularly powerful natural order. Here the cardinal points are not only inferred, but directly "visible", and human existence becomes part of a comprehensive and seemingly absolute system. Transitions and nuances are also lacking; everything has its precise meaning. The colours which in the Nordic world are pregnant with poetical possibilities, are here reduced to a few basic functions: white is sunlight, yellow-brown-grey the sand of the desert, blue the river, and green vegetation. These colours are applied to characterize things and places, such as the "artificial oasis" of the introvert dwelling. The most fundamental place structure of Khartoum in fact consists in the dialectical relationship between introvert dwelling and infinite but absolute environment.

But Khartoum is more. We have also emphasized its role as a meeting-place. In a meeting-place various spaces and characters are gathered to serve a complex form of life. Here the confluence of the Niles makes such a coming together natural. The quality of meeting-place is therefore not a historical product, but part of the basic place structure. Because of its potential significance as a centre, one would perhaps expect that the site had been chosen for a capital from early times. Most old centres, however, have developed as the focus of one particular civilization. Khartoum, instead, is located *between* the historical regions, in a kind of "no man's land". In this respect its location resembles that of Rome at the time of its foundation. Whereas the peoples which met in Rome lived close together within the same region, the confluence of the two Niles was far away from the particular foci of the surrounding civilization[8]. Khartoum therefore had to wait for the great international movements of Islam and European colonialism to assume its focal

role. The Three Towns make the focal role manifest, and their different character gives testimony to the cultural pluralism of present-day Sudan. At Khartoum, Arabic, African and European "forces" are gathered, a fact which is directly expressed by the colourful public life of the city. White, brown and black people in European, Arabic and African clothes mingle, and the languages spoken are legion. Although Khartoum is *different*, the visitor does not feel a stranger.

Whereas topological Omdurman represents the archetypal settlement in a desert world, the geometrical plan of Colonial Khartoum stems from a symbolization of the "cosmic" order described above. The plan, thus, comprises the coordinates of the compass as well as the directions of the Niles. Moreover it contains diagonals which correspond to the *qibla*. The artificial grid-iron hence becomes deeply meaningful in Khartoum, and we may suspect that it was chosen for this reason, rather than for its resemblance to the Union Jack. But although the use of an abstract symbolic form may help man to find a foothold within a comprehensive totality, it does not offer any guarantee for satisfactory dwelling in the everyday sense of the word. To solve this problem, porticoes were introduced which do not only offer climatic control, but also a concretization of the potential openness of the grid. The porticoes are thus accompanied by rhythmic arcades of indeterminate extension. Whereas the traditional local house is introvert, the colonial houses are extrovert, and express a different relationship between man and nature. Instead of retreat, we may talk about "conquest". In a desert world such a conquest remains an illusion, but the extrovert buildings anyhow make a continuous public

milieu possible, which allows for modern forms of human interaction.

In general the quality of place experienced in Khartoum stems from the meaningful interaction of natural and cultural "forces". The different cultural traditions are adapted to the local situation and get roots, while the natural site becomes part of a more comprehensive context. In this way Khartoum is a true place; local and universal at the same time. In existential terms we might say that the desert represents a *challenge* to man, with death as an ever present possibility. The river, however, introduces a *promise*, which through the appearance of vegetation becomes a real *hope*. This hope is concretized in human dwellings, that is, in the interior oases of the house of the Arabic-vernacular settlements and the arcaded and tree-lined streets of the colonial town. Finally, these solutions to the problem of dwelling are created within the general "cosmic" framework of the natural situation. Thus the "vocation" of Khartoum as a place is fulfilled, a fulfillment which is carried through down to the meaningful details of architectural articulation.

The historical "self-realization" of Khartoum started with the settlement at Tuti island. Being surrounded by water, Tuti does not ask man for any further retreat, but allows him to dwell within its "interior" space. Before any artificial oasis was created, Tuti was there, offering a fundamental lesson in the art of dwelling. The next step in the development followed when the villages of Omdurman, Khartoum and Khogali (North Khartoum) were founded at the end of the seventeenth century. Not only do they represent a propagation of the concept of dwelling "discovered" at Tuti, but they also define that three-polar structure which concretizes the general structure of the site. When

225. *The White Nile at sunset.*
226. *Meeting-place; black immigrants in Fallata,*
Khartoum South.

225. *The White Nile at sunset.*
226. *Meeting-place; black immigrants in Fallata, Khartoum South.*

Khartoum became the capital of Turco-Egyptian Sudan in 1823, its natural role as a centre was recognized. On geographical grounds Khartoum proper was chosen as the primary element within the conurbation. It is in fact situated between the Niles on the natural north-south axis. Judging from the old pictures in the *Illustrated London News*, the development of Khartoum happened without disturbing the general character of the habitat as a horizontally extended cluster of introvert compounds. When the Mahdi moved the capital to Omdurman in 1885, the role of the place as a spearhead of Arabic desert civilization was stressed, whereas Lord Kitchener's rebuilding of Khartoum represents a return to the "cosmopolitan" interpretation of the site. The last fundamental step in the definition of the place structure was taken with the ring of bridges which joins the Three Towns together to form an interacting, albeit differentiated totality (1909, 1929, 1963).

Our brief remarks show how the *genius loci* of the Khartoum conurbation was understood and respected in the past. In spite of the dramatic history of the place, its structure survived and was deliberately used and developed by the successive rulers. Today this structure is fairly well preserved, but the impact of the forces of "modern life" starts to make itself felt. The need for "planned development" thus induced the government of the Sudan to commission a master plan for the Three Towns from the Greek architect Doxiadis (1959). Without demonstrating the slightest understanding of the *genius loci*, Doxiadis placed an orthogonal grid over the whole conurbation, forcing the natural Gestalt as well as the various settlement structures into the same abstract straight-jacket.

Fortunately the plan has been recently

abandoned, and a plan more appropriate to the place is now being carried out[9], a plan which is based on an understanding of the geographical situation, the regional settlement pattern, the urban structure, and the local building typology and morphology; in short, on a respect for the *genius loci*.

1. Image

Rome is generally known as the "Eternal City". Obviously this name indicates something more than a very long history. To be "eternal" implies that the city has always conserved its *identity*. Rome, in fact, cannot be understood as a mere collection of relics from different periods. No explanation is needed to become aware of the "eternal" character of Roman architecture; it is immediately evident, whether we stand in front of a building from classical Antiquity or a Baroque structure. The "eternal" quality of Rome therefore resides in a very strong, perhaps unique, capacity for self-renewal. What, then, is this "self"? What is the *Idea romana* in architectural terms?

The common image of Rome is that of the great capital city, the *caput mundi* of Antiquity and the centre of the Universal Roman Catholic Church. In concrete terms this image implies monumentality and *grandezza*. And Rome is grandiose indeed, albeit not in the way we might have expected if we come from one of the many cities founded by the Romans in the various parts of the Empire. All these cities have the same lay-out, and we may recall the basic scheme: a pair of axes, the *cardo* and the *decumanus*, cross each other orthogonally within a regular quadrangle. The Roman city, thus, was distinguished by an abstract, "absolute" order, and because of this quality it served as a model for many capitals of later epochs. But Rome itself does not obey to any comprehensive geometrical system; from Antiquity on it always appeared as a large "cluster" of spaces and buildings of various size and shape. In Rome the absolute system of the crossing axes is confined to single elements, such as the *fora* and the *thermae*. A more comprehensive *axis urbis* may be found after a closer scrutiny[1], but it does not

227. *Model of Rome about 300 A.D., Museo
della Civiltà Romana.*

determine the immediate appearance of the city. It is therefore evident that the *genius loci* of Rome does not first of all reside in abstract order.

Perhaps it is rather determined by an extensive use of classical forms? As the capital of Antiquity, Rome ought to possess the harmonious equilibrium of classical architecture and its anthropomorphous presence. But Rome is quite different from a Greek city. The latter was distinguished by buildings which appeared as articulate bodies composed of "individual" members. The Roman building, on the contrary, was conceived as an integrated whole, as an enclosed space rather than a body. Moreover it was to a high extent assimilated by a superior urban totality. The classical Orders are there, but they do not have a constituent function. Evidently Rome cannot without reservations be characterized as a "classical" city. For a long time, in fact, Roman architecture was considered a degeneration of Greek architecture.

So far our question about the Roman *genius loci* remains unanswered. We feel its strong and "eternal" presence, but how should it be explained? Most valuable contributions to its understanding have been given by Kaschnitz von Weinberg and Kähler, but their investigations centred on grasping the varieties of classical architecture, rather than the character of Rome as a place[2]. Among the works of H. P. L'Orange, however, we find a profound and poetical description of Rome in phenomenological terms[3]. L'Orange does not take the single building as his point of departure, but wants to understand the urban environment as a whole. Thus he characterizes the Roman street with these words: "...the self-satisfied, enclosed world of the street is the characteristic quality of old Rome: a complete world, a small universe, an Eden from

which Nordic man is expelled; the *idyl* of the street, I should say"[4]. And he goes on describing the concrete properties of the Roman street, its enclosure and continuity which are determined by the lack of sidewalks and stairs in front of the entrances, its colours and smells, and its pulsating, multifarious life. The Roman street does not separate the houses, it unifies them, and gives you a feeling of being inside when you are out. The street is an "urban interior" where life takes place, in the full sense of the word. In the *piazza* this character is emphasized; the houses surround the space, and the centre is usually marked by a fountain. "The piazza may be planned or be a result of historical growth; always it crystallizes as an enclosed figure, always it is idyllically rounded"[5].

To use the world "idyl" to characterize the Roman *genius loci* may at first seem surprising. How can the capital of the world be "idyllic"? Obviously we do not have a kind of small-scale intimacy in mind, such as we find in the villages and towns of Denmark. Rome *is* monumental and grandiose, but at the same time its spaces have an "interiority" which give us a strong sense of protection and belonging. First of all, however, Rome has conserved a certain "rustic simplicity" which brings nature close. Hardly any other great European city expresses the same closeness to nature, and hardly any other place has in the same way *humanized* nature. This might be the essence of the Roman *genius loci*: the feeling of rootedness in a "known" natural environment. To understand Rome, we therefore have to leave the city and experience the surrounding landscape, the Roman *campagna*. The character of the campagna does not consist in "violent contrasts between forms, in a powerful juxtaposition of mass and space, mountain

142

and valley, but rather in a certain majestic and controlled rhythm in the articulation of the masses, in a subordination of the single figures to slowly rising or falling movements"[6]. Within the great unifying movements of the Roman landscape we may, however, discern several types which have their distinct and profoundly meaningful character. These landscapes are "gathered" by Rome; yes, it is the very existence of Rome which makes Latium become a unified whole.

Through an analysis of the landscapes of Latium we may threfore arrive at the needed explanation of the *genius loci* of Rome, of its various components and their interaction. First of all we have to travel to the strange, "sunken" valleys of Etruria, where "idyllic" spaces are closed in by continuous walls of golden-brown tufa. Originally the site of Rome had this character; the famous seven hills were not really hills but crests between a series of blind valleys along the Tiber. The Etruscans used the sides of such valleys for tombs and cellars, and built their villages on the crests. This was also the pattern of ancient Rome, and it constituted the truly *local* component of its *genius*. That its importance was recognized, is proved by the fact that the altar dedicated to the *genius loci* was located immediately under the steep tufa rock of the Palatine hill[7]. Secondly we have to visit the Alban hills on the other side of Rome, where we find a basically different landscape. Here the gods of Antiquity are at home, Jupiter, Juno and Diana, and the natural forms are in fact distinguished by "Greek" clarity and presence. Finally we should go to Palestrina, where the *cardo-decumanus* scheme for the first time was realized on a monumental scale. At Palestrina a "cosmic" order seems present in the landscape itself, and it is not surprising that the place was dedicated to the cult

234. *Lazio, diagrammatic map.*
235. *Forre at Chia.*

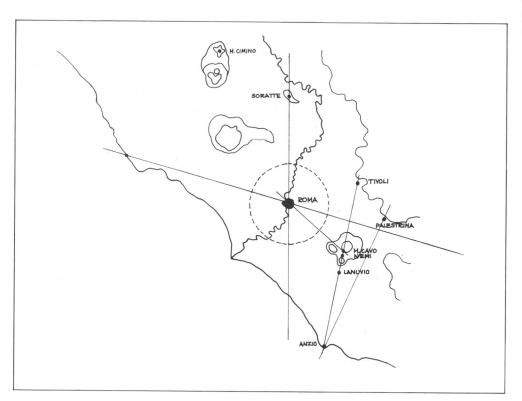

of Fortuna, that is, fate. After these excursions we may return to Rome with a basis for understanding its *genius loci*, and for explaining the meaning of the city as *caput mundi*.

2. Space

The Roman region is of volcanic origin. To the west and on both sides of the Tiber, the land is covered by a thick crust of old lava and ash which is known as *tufa*. During the millennia water courses have dug deep valleys and ravines in the volcanic crust, in Italian called *forre*[8]. The forre appear as surprising interruptions of the flat or rolling campagna, and as they are ramified and interconnected, they constitute a kind of "urban" netwoork of paths, a kind of "underworld" profoundly different from the everyday surface above. The campagna hardly offers other natural places; during the centuries the area around Rome had in fact an almost desert-like appearance. The forre therefore had a primary place-creating function, and innumerable villages have taken advantage of the protected and identified sites formed by the ramifications of the forre. (Sutri, Nepi, Civita Castellana, Barbarano, Vitorchiano, etc. etc.). In the forre one has the feeling of being "inside", a quality which is more often experienced in environments with a varied microstructure, than in the grand and perspicuous landscapes of the classical South. The forre have been extensively used during the course of history. In certain places (Norchia, Barbarano, Castel d'Asso) the Etruscans transformed the natural rocks into continuous rows of architectural façades, creating thus veritable cities for the dead. It is important to point out that the excavation of tufa rocks is an archetypal way of "building" in large parts of the Roman region. Today it is still a

236. *Vitorchiano.*

237. *Etruscan tomb at Veio, excavated in the tufa.*

238. *Forre at Norchia with etruscan rock-hewn facades.*

239. The Alban hills with Monte Cavo in the foreground and Lago di Nemi and Lanuvio in the background.
240. Mount Soracte.

241. The temple of Fortuna at Palestrina.
242. View from the temple of Fortuna.

well-known profession to be a *grottaiolo*, that is, an excavator of artificial caves. In general the forre bring us close to the ancient forces of the earth; they bring us "inside" and give us roots.

Whereas the landscape of the forre is *under* the "neutral" surface of the campagna, the Alban hills rise up to form an impressive and well delimited mass *over* the everyday world[9]. Being an old volcano, the Alban hills have a simple shape, and their clear topographical features are emphasized by the presence of two almost circular lakes in the deep craters. The hills thus possess the basic property of the classical landscape: a distinct and easily imageable relationship between masses and spaces. No wonder, hence, that the main sanctuaries of Latium were located here. On the top of Monte Cavo (*Albanus Mons*) Jupiter Latiaris presided over the whole region. In the woods on the slope of the mountains, Diana reigned, mirroring herself in the calm and deep Lago di Nemi, and on the other side of the lake, in Lanuvio (*Lanuvium*), where the slope is cultivated and less steep, Juno had her temple. It is hardly accidental that the sanctuaries are lined up on a north-south axis. Every spring the 47 members of the Latin confederation celebrated the *Feriae Latinae* on the top of Monte Cavo, confirming thus the importance of the Alban hills as the *centre* of the natural region of Latium. The hills in fact formed the nodal point for a system of sanctuaries. If we continue the "sacred axis" to the south, we reach Anzio (*Antium*) where there was a temple dedicated to Fortuna. Towards the north the same axis brings us to Tusculum where Castor and Pollux were at home, and to Tivoli (*Tibur*) where Hercules reigned over a wilder kind of environment. The main sanctuaries of Latium thus formed a natural *cardo* with Jupiter at the centre.

On the other side of Rome the situation was different; ancient Etruria was conquered by the Romans relatively late, and the wood-clad Monte Cimino for a long time remained an unsurmountable obstacle. Towards the north, however, where the Tiber valley reaches the Roman campagna, we find an isolated and very characteristic natural place, the mountain of Soracte, where the temple of the old sun-god Soranus was located, later to be identified with Apollo.

We understand that Rome is situated between two different worlds: to the west the chthonic world of the *forre*, and to the east the classical landscape of the gods. Around Rome, keeping both worlds at a certain distance, we find the campagna proper, which creates a kind of pause before one reaches the man-made synthesis of the city.

But this in not all. The third basic component of the Roman *genius loci*, the *cardo-decumanus* scheme, is also present in the natural surroundings. In Palestrina a large sanctuary dedicated to Fortuna was built about 80 B.C.[10]. Two old sacred places in the steep hillside were taken as the point of departure for the new lay-out: a circular temple of Fortuna Primigenia from the third century B.C., and a statue of Fortuna with Jupiter and Juno in her lap. These two elements were incorporated in a grand scheme of axially disposed terraces. The axis functions as a *cardo* which leads the eye between the Alban hills and the Lepine mountains towards the distant sea. Below the sanctuary the wide and fertile Sacco valley, which connects the Roman region with *Campania felix*, runs towards the east, crossing the north-south *cardo* like a *decumanus*.

Its direction is repeated in the terraces of the sanctuary, which thereby appears as a grandiose concretization of the "cosmic" order which embraces the whole landscape. When a Roman place was consecrated, the *augur* seated himself at the centre, and with his stick (*lituus*) he defined the two main axes, dividing space into four domains. This division represented the cardinal points, and the space which was thus articulated within the boundary of the horizon was called the *templum*. The sanctuary of Palestrina illustrates this procedure, and because of the correspondence between "cosmic" scheme and natural site it "proves" the validity of the scheme.

The seven hills of Rome do not suggest any cosmic order[11]. Rather irregularly five of them protrude from the campagna towards the Tiber, near the island which made the passage of the river easy. Between these hills and the Tiber two other tufa rocks rise more freely from the plain along the river, the Capitoline and the Palatine hills. Between all the hills a kind of basin is formed, which is the natural centre of the whole configuration. Further to the west a larger plain, the Campo Marzio, is embraced by the river. Being exposed and swampy, it remained outside the urban area until the second century B.C. On the other side of the Tiber the topographical conditions are simpler; a tufa ridge running north-south, the Janiculum, defines a smaller plain which in due time should become the suburb of Trastevere. The site of Rome, thus, belongs to the characteristic world of the *forre*. But it is not just one among many possible sites. Nowhere else along the Tiber an equally "strong" configuration is found, and in the whole of Etruria there hardly exists a similar cluster of hills, which is so well predisposed for a "conurbation". In early times Rome in fact consisted of several settlements, which, like the villages of present day Etruria, were located along the crests of the hills. Among these settlements, however, one had a par-

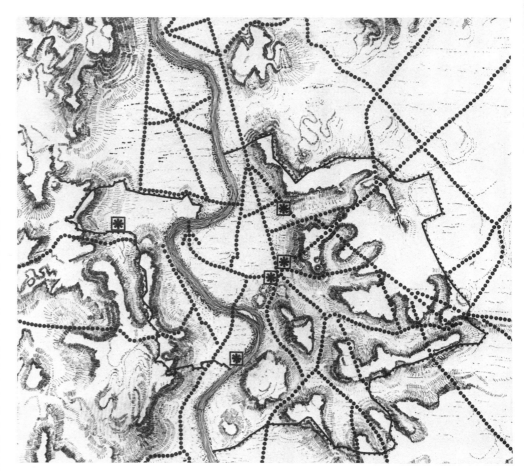

243. *The seven hills of Rome.*
244. *Axis urbis.*

245. *The Via Sacra with the Alban hills at the distance.*
246. *The "Centro Monumentale" of Antiquity. Model at the Museo della Civiltà Romana.*

ticular position and role: *Roma Quadrata* on the Palatine hill. According to legend this settlement was founded by Romulus and Remus in 753 B.C., and the name indicates that it might have possessed a *cardo* and a *decumanus*. The *axis urbis* of the conurbation, however, was the *Via Sacra* leading along the common *Forum* in the basin between the hills[12]. It is hardly a coincidence that this axis connects the Jupiter temple on the Capitol with the distant Alban hills! The *axis urbis* represents the first attempt to make Rome something more than a cluster of vernacular settlements. The fact that the axis symbolically extends towards the old centre of Latium, shows that the city wanted to assume the role of a true urban place which "gathers" the surroundings.

From early times, thus, Rome possessed a "double" spatial structure: the vernacular cluster of settlements with roots in the earth to which it belongs, and the abstract axis which made the city become the focus of a more comprehensive totality. The main property of the first component is the "idyllic" enclosure of the urban spaces, the second, instead, aims at axial symmetry. When these two components are combined, a particular kind of architectural unit comes into being: an axially ordered enclosure, which may be considered *the basic element* of Roman architecture. Ancient Rome literally consisted of such units serving various functions: fora, thermae, sanctuaries, palaces, atrium houses; all of them are axially ordered enclosures. It is important to note that the units conserve a certain independence within the urban totality. They are not assimilated by any superior geometrical system, but are "added" together like the individual buildings of the classical Greek settlement. Thus we arrive at the third fundamental property

247. *The plan of Pope Sixtus V. Fresco at the Vatican.*
248. *The trident of Piazza del Popolo.*

249, 250. *The Capitoline Square by Michelangelo.*

of Roman space: the classical image of an environment consisting of distinct, individual places. There is, however, one important difference: whereas the Greeks added up plastic "bodies", the Romans used *spaces* as units.

During the course of history the spatial structure of Rome was strenghtened and enriched. The "idyllic" enclosure was given ever new interpretations, but its basic importance was never doubted. A truly dominant system of streets was therefore impossible in Rome. The *axis urbis* of Antiquity was emphasized through the addition of new buildings, but it always remained implicit rather than explicit. First of all it got a centre when the Colosseum was built in the sacred valley between the hills (A.D. 75-80). The Colosseum certainly has a meaning which goes beyond its practical purpose. Its central location on the axis and its oval form suggest that it was intended as a "world theatre" where all the peoples under the rule of Rome could come together at the very centre of the Empire[13]. The *axis urbis* was moreover extended to the other side of the Tiber by the construction of a circus, where is the Vatican today (40 A.D.). Finally we may mention the temple of Venus and Rome (120 A.D.c.), which also stands on the axis. Having two *cellae* back to back, it visualizes the double extension of the axis which symbolized the role of Rome as *caput mundi*. The event of Christianity did not change the urban structure. As has been convincingly pointed out by Guidoni, Constantine transformed Rome symbolically into a Christian city by locating the two main churches on the *axis urbis*: the church of the Saviour (today St. John in the Lateran) to the south and St. Peter's to the north[14]. Later a symbolic "decumanus" was added between the churches of St. Paul and St. Mary (S. Maria

150

Maggiore), whereby the sign of the cross was put over the whole city. The centre of this cross was still the Colosseum, which was evidently accepted by the Christians as a cosmic symbol, a symbol whose fall would mean "the end of the world".

During the Renaissance and the Baroque several attempts were made to give Rome an integrated geometrical structure. The most radical and comprehensive changes were planned by Pope Sixtus V (1585-90)[15]. His principal aim was to connect the main religious foci of the city by means of wide, straight streets. Sixtus V integrated in his solution fragments of regular Renaissance planning carried out by his predecessors, in particular the trident of Piazza del Popolo, where three streets branch out to connect the main city gate with different urban districts. In general the plan of Sixtus V should make the individual sacred place become part of a comprehensive religious system. It is highly significant, however, that the plan remained a fragment. An abstract, superior system of the kind did not suit the Roman *genius loci*, and during the Baroque epoch, attention was again switched over to the creation of separate urban foci. The enclosed imperial fora of Antiquity were taken as a model, and a series of truly Roman spaces came into being.

The first, and urbanistically most significant urban interior was created already in the sixteenth century. The Capitoline Square by Michelangelo (1539 ff.) was intended as a new manifestation of Rome as *caput mundi*, that is as a central place which symbolized the role of Rome in the world[16]. But Michelangelo did not give the square an open, radiating lay-out as was normal at the time. Instead he made an enclosed space delimited by converging façades. A longitudinal axis was however introduced, which deprives the place of any self-sufficiency. The synthesis of enclosure and directed movement is concretized by the oval which is inscribed between the buildings. The star-shaped floor pattern of the oval creates a strong centrifugal movement which contrasts with the converging façades. Because of the simultaneous spatial expansion and contraction thereby obtained, the Capitoline Square becomes one of the greatest interpretations of the concept of place ever conceived by man. It brings us to the centre, not only of the world, but psychologically also of those departures and returns which constitute our individual existence.

The greatest of all Baroque squares, Piazza San Pietro by Bernini (1658-77), simply consists of a monumental colonnade which delimits an oval space[17]. The main axes of this oval are clearly defined and the centre is marked by an obelisk. Again, thus, we encounter the double theme of enclosure and direction, which has here been reduced to its very essentials. The colonnade encloses space in the simplest and most emphatic manner, and at the same time lets the "interior" communicate with the surrounding world. The basic spatial structure of Piazza San Pietro is strikingly similar to that of the Colosseum, and we may in this connection recall that Constantine substituted the Roman building with a round forum enclosed by colonnades when he planned Constantinople; a forum which had a nodal function analogous to that of the Colosseum. Piazza San Pietro has indeed become the new meeting place of all mankind, as was intended by Bernini, and it fulfills this function without giving up its Roman interiority.

It has been said that Rome is a city where one feels "inside" while being outside. The interiors of the main

251, 252. *Piazza San Pietro by Bernini.*
253. *The vaults of Constantine's Basilica.*
254. *Interior of the Pantheon.*

buildings make us experience this interiority in condensed form. The most important contribution of the ancient Romans to the history of architecture was in fact the creation of grand interior spaces and groups of such. In Greek architecture space is a mere "in-between", secondary to the surrounding buildings. In Rome, instead, it became the primary concern of architecture, and was treated as a "substance" to be shaped and articulated. Thus the spaces show a great variety of forms, and are covered by vaults and domes which so far had only played a secondary role in architecture. To make this possible, the Romans developed a new building technique, a kind of concrete which was cast to form continuous walls and coverings (*opus caementicium*). The Roman conception of interior space found its grandest manifestation in the Pantheon (A.D. 120), where a circular room is enclosed by a continuous, massive wall. The enclosure, however, is interpenetrated by a longitudinal axis, and thus the building visualizes the basic spatial properties of the Roman *genius loci*. In the Pantheon man's existence on earth is interpreted as "idyllic" sojourn *and* dynamic conquest, and both interpretations are made manifest under an "eternal", heavenly dome. In the Pantheon, thus, earth and heaven are united, and the Roman "idyl" is understood as the reflection of a general cosmic harmony. During the history of Roman architecture the same themes have been subject to ever new variations. Let us only mention the enclosed world of the Roman *palazzo*, the dialectic relationship between enclosure and axis in Michelangelo's St. Peter, and the High Baroque interpretation of the same themes in Borromini's Sant'Ivo.

3. Character

We have already pointed out that Rome

255. *"Roman" landscape at Civita Castellana.*
256. *Etruscan rock-hewn facades at San Giuliano, Viterbo.*

is located between two different "worlds": The chthonic world of Etruria and the classical world of the Alban hills, and we have implied that the urban environment reflects both of them. We have, however, also maintained that the natural site of the city rather belongs to the chthonic domain, and suggested that the streets and *piazze* of Rome have the forre of Etruria as their concrete model. In Vergil's Aeneid we find an illuminating description of the site: "Next Evander showed Aeneas a large grove which bold Romulus was later to make his sanctuary, and, under a dank crag, the Lupercal, the Wolf's Cave, which is named in the Arcadian fashion after the Wolf-god, Lycaean Pan. He showed him also the sacred grove of the Argiletum, and explained how on this spot Argos met his death, although a guest. From there he conducted him to the Tarpeian Rock and the Capitol, which is now all gold, but which was once wild and convered with undergrowth. Even in those days that spot held a sinister awe of its own, which inspired fear and dread in the country folk, who trembled at the trees and the rocks. Evander continued: "This hill with its wooded crest is the abode of some god, but it is not known which god he is. The Arcadians believe they have seen Jupiter here, shaking the dark aegis in his right hand to gather the clouds of storm"[18]. And, indeed, Jupiter got his temple on the Capitoline hill, from where he tamed the occult forces of rocks and woods. The passage from Vergil is highly significant as it makes the original *genius loci* become alive. Today the rocks and hills of Rome have lost most of their presence, as the ground has risen 10-20 metres during the course of history, and we have to go to Etruria to rediscover the landscape which "educated the eyes" of the ancient Romans. In the forre of Etruria we meet

154

what Paolo Portoghesi appropriately has called "Rome before Rome"[19]. Here we find the golden-brown colour of Piazza Navona and the Roman streets, and we find the soft, malleable tufa which has determined the Roman sense of form. Although the landscape of the forre has some properties in common with the romantic landscapes of the Nordic countries, it is basically different. The forre do not constitute any infinite, mysterious world such as the Nordic forest, but consist of delimited imageable spaces. And their relationship to the sky is also different. The walls of the forre do not end in a serrate silhoutte, but are suddenly cut off by the flat campagna. Thus they end like a row of buildings crowned by a cornice. The Etruscans in fact transformed the walls into semi-classical façades (Norchia). Rather than being a romantic world in the Nordic sense, the forre therefore represent a "pre-classical" world, a world which still waits for being humanized.

The vernacular architecture of the Roman region is closely related to its natural character. The houses usually have a simple prismatic shape with a sloping roof which hardly projects beyond the wall. Mostly they are joined together in such a way, however, that it is not easy to distinguish the single units. The general character is massive and enclosed; the windows are small and are cut into the walls like holes. The most common building material is tufa blocks, whose colour may vary from dark brown to yellow, grey and black. The softness of the material and the rather irregular joining of the blocks make the buildings seem "modelled" rather than "built", an impression which is stressed by the continuous but irregular rows of facades. Rising up from rocks of tufa, the houses appear as a more precise version of the natural forms, and usually the villages are

258. *Rome before the Lungotevere was built.*

259. *Old street in the Ghetto.*
260. *Via Biberatica, forum of Trajan.*
261. *Via del Governo Vecchio.*

262. *Palazzo della Cancelleria.*
263. *Palazzo Massimo by Peruzzi.*
264. *Palazzo Farnese by A. da Sangallo and Michelangelo.*
265. *Palazzo di Propaganda Fide by Borromini.*

located in such a way that they define and emphasize important structural features in the landscape, such as crests, isolated plateaus, and "promontories". When architecture is used to clarify and visualize a landscape which consists of imageable forms and spaces, it is appropriate to talk about a "pre-classical" character, a quality which is emphasized by the elementary shape of the houses themselves. The vernacular architecture of the Roman region thus combines closeness to the earth with a wish for imageable order.

The urban architecture of Rome to a high extent conserves this vernacular character. On the Campo Marzio and especially in Trastevere the streets often look like hollowed-out spaces in tufa rocks rather than "built" environments; an impression which is strengthened by the heavy and rusticated ground-floors. The arched openings of the *tabernae* remind us of the grottoes excavated in the walls of the *forre*. The arches themselves rarely have a tectonic appearance; usually they form an integral part of a continuous, "modelled" frame around the opening. The building materials, very thin bricks and plaster, emphasize the general continuity of the space-defining boundaries. In the simpler houses articulation is scarce. Mostly it only consists in a subdivision of the façade by means of string-courses. In more articulate buildings, the floors may be differentiated among themselves; for instance by making them gradually "lighter" over a rusticated base. We may in this context recall Serlio's characterization of the rusticated wall as *opera di natura*, a concept which proves that the architecture of the *cinquecento* still recognized its vernacular roots. The differentiation of the storeys, however, never becomes a vertical "addition" of independent units. The classical Orders are usually absent from Roman secular

façades, but classical detail appears as pediments, cornices etc. The traditional Roman house is therefore a unified and enclosed building, characterized by plasticity and heaviness. The architectural detail is applied to a massive core, rather than being part of an articulate body. The type has conserved its identity throughout the course of history. We find it in the *insulae* of ancient Rome, as is clearly evident in the better preserved sections of Ostia and in the "Via Biberatica" in Rome. It remained alive during the Middle Ages[20], and reappeared with full force in the palaces of the Renaissance and the Baroque.

The classical superimposition of Orders introduced by Alberti in Palazzo Rucellai, Florence, about 1450, never became a success in Rome. After the use of façade-pilasters in the Cancelleria (1489ff.) Roman architecture returned to the massive *opera di natura*, an approach which found its typical manifestation in Palazzo Farnese by Antonio da Sangallo (1517ff.). Thus the Roman environment conserved its closeness to nature. Even during the Baroque period the palace did not change its basic properties. A building such as Borromini's Palazzo di Propaganda Fide (1647ff.) appears as a large, enclosed mass. The rounded corners emphasize its plastic character, and the string-courses between the storeys tie the volume together rather than subdivide it. The entrance façade shows a convex-concave movement which makes the continuity of the Roman wall evident. The row of giant plasters which flank the main gate, do not belong to any skeletal structure, but, together with the elaborate windows on the main floor, visualizes the "archaic" plastic force of the building. Evidently, thus, the classical members have a particular function in Roman architecture.

In Greek architecture the classical mem-

268. *The Palazzo dei Conservatori by Michelangelo.*
269. *Santa Costanza, interior.*

bers are constituent elements in the full sense of the word. The buildings are *made* of columns, entablature and pediments. They are "trabeated structures", where each member embodies the character of the whole. In Roman architecture, instead, the classical Orders are applied to or "liberate" themselves from a mass which is "given" *a priori*. The Orders therefore have a purely characterizing function, and are used to "humanize" the given *opera di natura*. This is already evident in the Colosseum, where the superimposed Orders transform the primary mass into a *system* of characters. Being a main public building, a "centre" where the structure of existence becomes manifest, the Colosseum exposes the Orders *outside*, and thereby it fulfills its focal role in the urban environment. In the Roman palace, instead, the superimposition of Orders is confined to the *cortile*. The ancient forces of nature dominate the exterior, and we have to go inside to find the human world of the classical characters. In the courtyard man has freed himself from the domination of the *genius loci*, and may live with those forms which symbolize his general understanding of the world. The classical *aedicola* which is used to mark the entrance to the palace, announces the character of this interior domain.

In certain cases, however, the Orders are also used to characterize a public, urban space. As examples we may again quote the Capitoline Square and Piazza San Pietro. Being main urban foci, these squares represent a synthesis of nature and culture. They "gather" the meanings of the particular natural environment as well as man's general knowledge, and thereby make a total form of life visible. In both cases this problem is solved in a truly Roman way. The squares are not only "urban interiors", but their boundaries have the plastic quality and

"grandezza" of the typical Roman wall. A giant order is used (pilasters at the *Campidoglio* and columns at St. Peter's) which carries a very heavy entablature crowned by a balustrade and a row of statues. The powerful interaction of vertical and horizontal members is Roman rather than Greek, and when we walk inside the colonnade of Piazza San Pietro between the immense, swelling Tuscan shafts, we feel an echo of the ancient world of the *forre* and remember Vergil's words about the "sinister awe" of the Roman environment. Here this awe does not announce the presence of Jupiter, but prepares for entering the church of St. Peter's, perhaps the greatest manifestation of Roman "interiority" after the Pantheon.

Since the first churches were built under Constantine, Roman sacred architecture has conserved its typical properties. The basic themes of enclosure and axiality were from the very beginning concretized in centralized and longitudinal structures, which were used as baptistry/tomb and congregational basilica respectively, a profoundly meaningful distinction which interprets life as a "path" between birth and death[21]. In both cases the early church was distinguished by a strong "interiority". The exterior was hardly given any architectural attention, except for a certain emphasis on the main façade; it was conceived as a neutral shell around a richly articulate interior. In general this theme is taken over from Antiquity, but the Christian interpretation is different. The interior of the Pantheon is evidently a representation of the cosmos. The space is divided in three superimposed zones; the first having a plastic character, the second a simpler and more regular articulation, whereas the geometrical dome, makes eternal harmony manifest. In the Early Christian church we find an echo of this differentiation;

272. *Piazza Navona.*
273. *Piazza Navona with fountain by Bernini.*

274. *The Spanish Steps.*

275. *Piazza San Pietro, colonnade by Bernini.*
276. *The Trevi fountain.*

but the precise anthropomorphous character of the lower zone is subdued, while the upper part of the space is transformed into a de-materialized heavenly domain which spreads out as continuous surfaces of shimmering mosaic.

The churches of the Renaissance and the Baroque offer new interpretations of the same themes. Again we find that the exterior is of secondary importance, except for an increasing emphasis on the main façade, which in the Baroque churches indicates a return to the more active relationship between the exterior and interior world of ancient Roman architecture. Only the domes which rise over the roofs of the surrounding houses, are fully articulate bodily forms which signalize the urban presence of the values symbolized by the church. These domes are also eminently Roman in their harmonious equilibrium of horizontal and vertical "movements"; so basically different from the "aspiring" silhouettes of Byzantine and Eastern churches. In the interiors of the Roman Baroque the antropomorphous members of classical architecture are again used with full assurance. Even the tiny space of S. Carlino by Borromini (1639ff.) is surrounded by a "colonnade" of plastic shafts, and in St. John in the Lateran the same architect used a rhythmical succession of giant pilasters. In general, however, the Baroque churches conserve the primeval cave-like character of Roman space, and shun the Gothic inspired de-materialization of Central European buildings[22].

The Romans did to space what the Greeks did to plastic form. Applying the classical orders to the boundaries of interiors and urban spaces, they transformed the amorphous enclosure into a structured whole where the properties of the boundaries determine the character of the space. Although it is hardly

possible to give the boundary of a space the same presence as a bodily form, walls may be transformed into a plastic skeleton, as was done by Bernini in the colonnade of St. Peter's Square. The "normal" Roman solution, however, was to *apply* the classical members to a continuous, structural wall. This is the method used in the Pantheon, the great *thermae*, the Basilica of Maxentius as well as the Baroque churches. What is "given" in Roman architecture is therefore mass and space as primeval totalities. "The man who excavates a space in the soft rock, does not construct an "opposite" which, like the Greek temple, faces him… . He rather penetrates into amorphous matter, and his creative activity consists in making for himself an existential space"[23]. These words of Kaschnitz von Weinberg well define the different approaches of the Greeks and the Romans. We only have to add that the Romans took over the classical orders to "humanize" their existential space.

To conclude we might visit Piazza Navona, were we encounter the existential space of the Romans in its archetypal form. Piazza Navona is not a monumental square; here we rather return to the origins, and rediscover the "idyllic" world of the forre and the vernacular settlements. Its general properties concretize the local landscape, and its continuous orange-brown walls make us remember the tufa of Etruria. The articulation of the boundaries however, also comprises the antropomorphous Classical characters, with the dome of S. Agnese as a primary, bodily manifestation. None of the two components dominate, an ideal equilibrium between nature and culture has been achieved. At Piazza Navona we are really "inside", close to the earth, close to the palpable things of everyday existence, at the same time as we feel

part of a comprehensive cultural totality. No wonder that it has become the popular place of Rome *par excellence*. The synthesis of nature and culture is condensed and visualized in Bernini's great fountain, where natural elements such as water and rocks are combined with human figures and religious symbols, as well as the *axis mundi* of the obelisk. In front of the church of S. Agnese, finally, we find another characteristic Roman element: a broad flight of stairs. In Rome, stairs are not used to create a distance betweeen different existential realms; rather they represent an articulation of the ground itself. The great Roman stairs bring us close to the earth and increase our sense of belonging to the place.

4. Genius Loci

Our analysis of the spatial structure and character of the Roman region has shown that Rome forms the centre of a landscape which contains "everything". In Latium the old chthonic forces are present, as well as the anthropomorphous characters of the classical gods, and the abstract, cosmic order of the sky. These meanings become manifest as an exceptionally varied and rich environment. In Etruria we encounter the "underworld" of the forre, in the Alban hills we rise up to meet the "new" gods, and between these two realms the campagna forms an everyday level where the daily life of man takes place. The role of Rome as *caput mundi* is undoubtedly determined by this natural situation. In Rome all the basic categories of existential meanings are gathered, like in no other place. This gathering does not simply consist in the central location of the city, but in an active symbolization of the various meanings. The world of the forre is thus reproduced in the streets and *piazze* of Rome's everyday environment, and the

gods are brought down from the hills to be housed in urban temples. From these temples they extend their influence to the whole environment: classical forms appear on the façades and in the courtyards of the houses and palaces, and "humanize" their "natural" structure. This synthesis of the chthonic and the classical constitutes the essence of the Roman "idyl". In the Greek towns instead, the chthonic forces were vanquished by the "new" gods, and the environment became fully classical. What was thereby gained in human content, was lost as a separation from the given natural reality.

The Roman synthesis also comprises the cosmic dimension which from immemorial times has been associated with the course of the sun. Straight north of Rome, Soracte rises up to receive its rays: "Look how the snow lies deeply on glittering Soracte…" says Horace[24], and still today the mountain exercises its spell on the visitor of the campagna. The quality of the light is certainly one of the great environmental factors which have determined the Roman *genius loci*. In Rome it has neither the thing-consuming force of the desert sun, nor the shimmering atmospheric quality encountered in the North. The Roman light is strong and reliable, it brings out the plastic quality of things, and when it meets the golden-brown tufa, the environment gets a warm and assuring character. But the cosmic dimension is something more than light. First of all it implies a system of directions which forms a frame of reference for all appearances. The cardinal points give man a general foothold in a mutable world. They are not tied to any particular place, but have a universal validity which made the *cardo-decumanus* scheme the natural symbol of the Roman Empire[25]. It would be near-sighted to interpret the scheme as a mere

expression of power; it rather concretizes the belief in a general cosmic harmony behind all phenomena. With the incorporation of the cardinal points in all the main building types, the Roman synthesis became complete.

In Palestrina this synthesis got its concrete confirmation. Here *nature itself* reveals its hidden order, and only asks man to make it more clearly manifest through building. In the Colosseum and the Pantheon the synthesis becomes symbolically present in the urban *man-made* environment. The Colosseum thus unifies primeval matter, anthropomorphic Orders and cosmic axes in the simplest possible way. Being the urban focus of Rome, it reveals this synthesis openly "in public". The Pantheon instead, makes the same meanings manifest as an "interior" world, expressing thereby that the Roman synthesis is not something man has superimposed on the world. It is inherent in the world, and if we penetrate into things, we shall discover truth. Both buildings make us remember Heidegger's words that "to be on earth means to be under the sky". The Colosseum is open in the vertical direction and is covered by the sky itself. When you are inside, the irregular "profane" horizon of the city is left behind; a perfect, undisturbed contour forms the basis for the natural dome above. Never has man made the sky present in a more convincing way[26]. In the Pantheon the world is gathered under a built, symbolic dome. It is important to note that the coffers of the dome are not related to the centre of the sphere which could be inscribed within the space. The dome is related to the centre of the floor, that is, to the centre of the earth, and the vertical axis which rises up from this centre through the large opening in zenit, therefore unifies earth and heaven (also as light) in a meaningful totality.

The architecture of Rome gathers and visualizes a "complete" environment. This gathering obviously comprises influences from other cultures. Thus Goethe said that Rome "gave a dwelling to all gods". These influences, however, did not remain a mere foreign import; thanks to the multifarious structure of Latium, almost everything found a local reference. If the Alban hills had not been there, the classical gods would not have been really at home in Rome, and if the campagna had not possessed its grand and solemn structure, the image of a general cosmic order might only have seemed a far-fetched product of the human imagination. This general receptivity is the real meaning of the saying that "all roads lead to Rome". We might add that they also lead *from* Rome.

The power and versatility of the Roman *genius loci* has throughout history given the architecture of the city a unique self-assurance and *grandezza*. Even the pure and elegant *quattrocento* got a new substantiality under the influence of Roman Antiquity. A great unified *interior* such as Alberti's Sant'Andrea in Mantua is unthinkable without Rome, and its façade reproduces the Roman triumphal arch. The crisis of the *cinquecento* did not reduce Roman architecture to an arbitrary play with forms, as it did in other places. In Rome it rather brought about a resurrection of the chthonic forces. This is particularly evident in the villas of Bagnaia, Bomarzo and Tivoli, where man really returns to nature. It is in this connection interesting to note that the *cinquecento* preferred the "wild" nature of Etruria and Tivoli to the classical environment of Frascati, which instead became the fashionable place of the *seicento*. Still more important is the fact that even the tragic art of Michelangelo respects the Roman *genius loci*. The strong plasticity and immense heaviness of his bodies is truly Roman,

and when he defines the body as the "prison of the soul", he interprets the local spirit relative to his own situation. Michelangelo's art thus remains within the Roman limits: it never becomes unsubstantially abstract like Nordic Mannerism. During the Baroque period the *genius loci* and the spirit of the time fitted perfectly together. Both wanted a comprehensive, triumphant synthesis, and the result was the exuberant works of Bernini and the integrated and dynamic spaces of Borromini. The complex personality of the latter certainly reflects a multitude of "influences" and a certain "romantic" approach to architecture, but his conception of space as an enclosed, indivisible unit, remains essentially Roman. Rather than being antagonists, Bernini and Borromini therefore offered different interpretations of the same local character.

Rome has conserved its identity down to our time. During the Fascist period a serious attack on the "idyllic" coherence of the city was carried out, but it was stopped in time. Unfortunately actual construction does not show much understanding for the *genius loci* either. Only in the Sports Palaces by Nervi do we still feel the Roman sense of space and plastic presence[27]. More dangerous than the new buildings, however, is the gradual destruction of the landscape of Latium. In the past a destroyed Rome meant a return to nature; for centuries the ruins of past civilizations were the distinctive mark of the Roman landscape. From this nature Rome was always reborn as Rome, but today the soil which gave the place its identity is becoming a mere memory. The Colosseum is still standing, but man obviously does not any more respect the *meanings* it embodies. Perhaps the fall of Colosseum was meant in this metaphorical sense!

1. Meaning

To arrive at an understading of the *genius loci*, we have introduced the concepts of "meaning" and "structure". The "meaning" of any object consists in its relationships to other objects, that is, it consists in what the object "gathers". A thing is a thing by virtue of its gathering. "Structure", instead, denotes the formal properties of a system of relationships. Structure ad meaning are hence aspects of the same totality[1]. Both are abstractions from the flux of phenomena; not in the sense of scientific classification, but as a direct recognition of "constancies", that is, stable relationships which stand out from the more transitory happenings. The child's "construction of reality" implies that it has learnt to perceive changing phenomena as representing the same thing[2], and comprises the basic concepts of "object", "spatial field" and "temporal field"[3], which correspond to our categories "thing", "order" and "time". This means that every child so to speak repeats the process of understanding which is reflected in the ancient cosmologies. It goes without saying that the child also develops an understanding of the expression or character of the objects perceived, in relation to its own psychic structure. In fact, children, like "primitive" people, do not distinguish the psychic from the physical, and experience things as "animate"[4]. In general, meaning is a *psychic* function. It depends on *identification*, and implies a sense of "belonging". It therefore constitutes the basis of dwelling. We ought to repeat that man's most fundamental need is to experience his existence as meaningful.

When discussing the natural and man-made place, we gave a general survey of their basic meanings and structural properties. The natural meanings were grouped in five categories, which sum

279. *Place; enclosure and gathering.*
Monteriggioni, Toscana.

up man's understanding of nature. Evidently man interacts with these meanings. He is a "thing" among "things": he lives among mountains and rocks, rivers and trees; he "uses" then and has to know them. He also lives with the "cosmic order": with the course of the sun and the cardinal points. The directions of the compass are not mere geometry, but qualitative realities which follow man everywhere. In particular, man is related to the "character" of things. From the initial animistic stage he gradually develops a conscious or unconscious understanding that there exists an *Übereinstimmung*, a correspondence, between his own psychic states and the "forces" of nature. Only thus he may obtain a personal "friendship" with things, and experience the environment as meaningful. He cannot be friends with scientific "data", but only with qualities. Man also lives with "light" and is tuned by light. Personal and collective attitudes ("mentalities") are in fact influenced by the environmental "climate"[5]. Finally man lives in "time", which means that he lives with the changes of the other four dimensions. He lives with the rhythms of day and night, with the seasons and in history.

Man's dependence on nature has long been recognized. Hegel starts his "Philosophy of History" with a chapter on the "Geographic Basis of World History", and wants to define the "natural type of the locality, which is closely related to the type and character of the people which is born from this soil. This character is the way peoples appear and find their place in world history"[6]. Herder introduced the concept "climate" to cover the entire natural and man-made environment, and characterized man's life as "climatic". He added, however, that climate does not "force" man; rather it "tends" and "disposes"[7].

Arnold Toynbee interpreted the relationship between man and his environment as a "challenge and response"[8]. To a high extent Toynbee understands "environment" as physical nature. All these great historians thus recognized the importance of the natural environment, but simultaneously they stressed man's ability to "respond" and to shape his world. Man does not obviously only "build" nature, but also builds himself, society and culture, and in this process he may interpret a given environment in different ways.

The relationship between man and nature also forms a point of departure for Marx. It is a basic tenet of Marxism that man as a biological being is part of nature, and that nature is an "objective reality", which is given independently of man's consciousness. Man faces this reality in his work, and thus realizes his purposes "in nature". This implies that he may "master" nature, without however isolating himself from it. Rather he ought to arrive at an ever deeper understanding of its "laws". Man's consciousness is both in its content and form a "reflection" of nature, although it possesses a certain independence and power of feedback. To understand Marxism, however, it is essential to add that it defines nature as *matter*. "Matter" is used as a simultaneously very wide and concrete concept ("matter as such does not exist, only its concrete manifestations"), but it does not cover our concepts of "meaning" and "character". Although structurally sound, as regards the relationship between man and his environment, Marxism therefore remains incomplete. The psychological aspect is left out, that is, the functions of orientation and identification. Because of this omission, Marxism does not arrive at a full understanding of "dwelling", and fails in its attempt to win human alienation[9].

Alienation is in our opinion first of all due to man's loss of identification with the natural and man-made things which constitute his environment. This loss also hinders the process of gathering, and is therefore at the root of our actual "loss of place". Things have become mere objects of consumption which are thrown away after use, and nature in general is treated as a "resource"[10]. Only if man regains his ability of identification and gathering, we may stop this destructive development. The first step to take is to arrive at a full understanding of the *objects* of identification and gathering, that is, an understanding of the concept of *thing*. Thereby we shall also be able to define the nature of man-made meanings and their relation to natural meanings. Again we have to ask Heidegger for help. In his essay *The Thing*, he uses a jug as example, and asks for the "jugness" of the jug. "The jug's jug-character consists in the poured gift of the pouring out... The giving of the outpouring can be a drink. The spring stays on in the water of the gift. In the spring the rock dwells, and in the rock dwells the dark slumbers of the earth, which receives the rain and the dew of the sky. In the water of the spring dwells the marriage of sky and earth... In the gift of water, in the gift of wine, sky and earth dwell. But the gift of the outpouring is what makes the jug a jug. In the jugness of the jug, sky and earth dwell..." "The jug's essential nature, its presencing... is what we call a thing"[11]. Heidegger takes the function of the jug, the pouring, as his point of departure. He defines the pouring as a gift and asks what is here "given". Water and wine are given, and with them earth and sky. The jug is understood as an artifact which serves a purpose. Its function, however, forms part of a life which takes place between earth and sky. The jug participates in

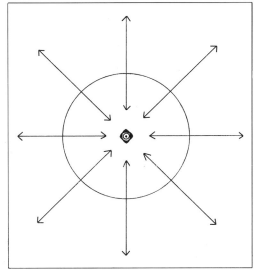

this taking place; yes, *it is part of the place* in which life is concretized. The function of real things is therefore to concretize or "reveal" life in its various aspects. If a thing does not do that, it is not a thing but a mere commodity. We dwell poetically when we are able to "read" the revealing of the things which make up our environment. Things are made with the purpose of revealing; they gather world, and may themselves be gathered to form a microcosmos.

What, then, does this tell us about the nature of man-made things? Are they only reflections of natural meanings, or does man create meanings of his own? Have we not already shown that the meanings of man-made place are determined by economic, social, political, and other cultural phenomena? Heidegger's example, however, implies that man cannot create meanings that are *entirely* his own. Man is part of a living world, and does not conceive meanings in a vacuum. Meanings necessarily form part of a totality, which comprises natural components. Everything created by man is *in* the world, it is between earth and sky, and has to make this state of affairs manifest. In doing this, the created thing gets roots in a locality or at least in nature in general. Our categories "romantic architecture", "cosmic architecture" and "classical architecture" denote different modes of being rooted in nature.

But the function of man-made things (places) goes beyond the manifestation of simple rootedness. The concept of gathering implies that natural meanings are brought together in a *new* way, in relation to human purposes. Natural meanings are thus abstracted from their natural context, and as elements of a language they are com-posed to form a "new", complex meaning which illuminates nature as well as man's role within the totality[12]. Evidently such a composition may also comprise elements which are *invented* by man. We have already mentioned how man makes a land-mark or a house, which *a posteriori* are used to "understand" his environment. To be meaningful, however, the inventions of man must have formal properties which are structurally similar to other aspects of reality, and ultimately to natural structures. If this is not the case, they would isolate themselves within a purely artificial world, and lose contact with reality. The basic kinds of structural similarity ought to be described in terms of our categories "space" and "character". Natural and man-made space are structurally similar as regards directions and boundaries. In both, the distinction between up and down is valid, as well as the concepts of extension and enclosure. The boundaries of both kinds of space are moreover to be defined in terms of "floor", "wall", and "ceiling". Natural and man-made space may thus *represent* each other reciprocally. The same holds true for natural and human characters, as was understood by the Greeks. The man-made forms which concretize characters obviously do not *imitate* the analogous natural forms, but we have again to ask for common structural properties.

"Gathering" means that things are brought together, that is, that they are moved from one place to another. This transposition is in general done by means of symbolization, but it may also consist in a concrete displacement of buildings and things. Whereas moving by means of symbolization is a creative act of interpretation and translation, concrete displacement is passive, and mostly connected with the wish for getting a "cultural alibi"[13]. The Greek *polis* was based on a creative transposition of meanings. The meanings which are revealed in certain natural places, were translated into buildings

282. System of rivers.
283. Valley settlements, diagram.
284. Norwegian farm. Harildstad, Heidal.

and moved to the city, through the erection of similar buildings there. It is a grand conception, indeed, to visualize the qualities of a landscape by means of a man-made structure, and then to gather several landscapes symbolically in one place! We have seen that the *genius loci* of Rome stems from such a gathering.

Obviously meanings are moved because they are of *general* interest, that is, because they are part of "truth". The symbols which make truth manifest constitute *culture*. Culture means to transform the given "forces" into meanings which may be moved to another place. Culture is therefore based on abstraction and concretization. By means of culture man gets rooted in reality, at the same time as he is freed from complete dependence on a particular situation. We understand that the given economic, social, political and cultural conditions do not *produce* the meanings concretized by a man-made place[14]. The meanings are inherent in the world, and are in each case to a high extent derived from the locality as a particular manifestation of "world". The meanings may however be *used* by the economic, social, political and cultural forces. This use consists in *a selection among possible meanings*. The selection therefore tells us about the actual conditions, but the meanings as such have deeper roots. In general they are covered by our four categories "thing", "order", "character" and "light". Traditionally these categories have been associated with earth, sky, man and spirit, respectively. They thus correspond to what Heidegger calls the "fourfold" (*das Geviert*)[15]. Dwelling consists in "preserving" the fourfold, which in general means to "keep the fourfold in that with which mortals stay: in things"[16]. The nature of a thing resides in its gathering. The jug gathers earth

and sky, and the bridge gathers the earth as landscape around the stream. In general things gather world and thereby reveal truth. To make a thing means the "setting-into-work" of truth. A place is such a thing, and as such it is a poetical fact.

The making of places we call architecture. Through building man gives meanings concrete presence, and he gathers buildings to visualize and symbolize his form of life as a totality. Thus his everyday lifeworld becomes a meaningful home where he can dwell. There are many kinds of buildings and settlements. What they gather varies according to the building task and the situation. Vernacular architecture, that is, farms and villages, brings the immediate meanings of the local earth and sky into presence. Hence it is "circumstantial" and intimately connected with a particular situation. Urban architecture, instead, has a more general value, as it is based on symbolization and transposition[17]. Urban architecture therefore presupposes a formal language, a "style". In the town, "foreign" meanings meet the local *genius*, and create a more complex system of meanings. The urban *genius* is never merely local; although the examples of Prague, Khartoum and Rome have taught us that the local character plays a decisive role in giving the settlement its particular identity. Urban gathering may be understood as an *interpretation* of the local *genius*, in accordance with the values and need of the actual society. In general we may say that *the meanings which are gathered by a place constitute its genius loci*.

Architecture is born from the dialectic of departure and return. Man, the wanderer, is on his way. His task is to penetrate the world and to set its meanings into work. This is the meaning of the word *settle*. A settlement sets

truth into a work of architecture. To set-into-work here means to build the boundary or "threshold" from which the settlement begins its presencing. The threshold is the meeting of "outside" and "inside", and architecture is hence the *incarnation* of the meeting. "The place-searching and place-forming characters of plastic incarnation"[18] here find their "look" and at the same time man finds his "outlook"[19]. Thus the threshold is the "gathering middle"[20], where things appear in "limpid brightness".

2. Identity

Places where natural and man-made elements form a synthesis are the subject-matter of a phenomenology of architecture. The primary relationship between the two kinds of elements is denoted by the world *location*. Where does man locate his settlements? Where does nature form places which "invite" man to settle? The question has to be answered both in terms of space and character. From the spatial point of view man needs an enclosure, and accordingly tends to settle where nature offers a defined space. From the point of view of character, a natural place which comprises several meaningful things, such as rocks, trees and water, would represent an "invitation". We have in fact seen that Rome was founded in a place where these elements were present. Some times the conditions may be favourable both with regard to space and character, other times only one of the two needs is naturally satisfied (or even none). Where the actual conditions are favourable, visualization becomes the most important means of place concretization, whereas a location where nature offers less, has to be "improved" by complementation and symbolization[21].

In a very general sense, the surface relief of the earth slopes down towards the

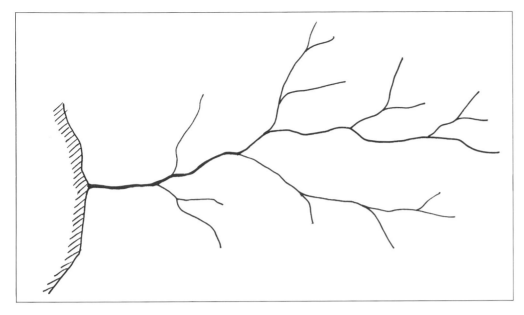

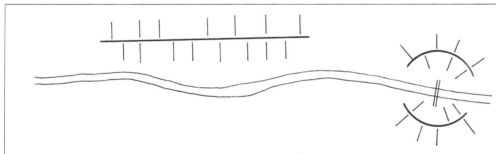

sea. Except for a few isolated internal basins (possibly of volcanic origin), a "normal" country is always directed towards the sea[22]. On an extended plain this direction is obviously less strongly felt than in a valley. In general, the movement of the land corresponds to a system of rivers (and lakes) which visualize the spatial pattern. When the river approaches the sea, the valley usually opens up and becomes an amphitheatrical bay. The location of human settlements are to a high extent determined by these conditions. Spaces such as plains, valleys and bays have given rise to characteristic types of settlements, and mostly a river, a confluence, or a shore have been used for spatial fixation. The endings of numerous place names express this state of affairs: "ford", "port", "mouth", "gate", "haven", "bridge". When the surface relief of a hill landscape gets accentuated, however, the natural places are found on the tops and crests of the hills rather than in the bottom of the valleys. We see thus that the scale of the surface relief may influence location. A top is obviously also often chosen because it forms a natural centre to the surrounding landscape. Another general factor which influences location is the direction of the sun. A slope exposed to the south is evidently more favourable than a northern one, and in many parts of Europe it is therefore common that farms and villages are situated on the north side of the valleys. Sometimes exposure and natural space collaborate to create very favourable conditions for settlement, other times they are contradictory and some kind of compromise becomes necessary.

If man-made places are at all related to their environment, there ought to exist a meaningful correspondence between natural conditions and *settlement morphology*. The basic problem to be solved

by a settlement is how to gather the surrounding landscape. How do we, in terms of space, gather a plain, a valley, an undulating series of hills, or a bay? Evidently, each of these situations are open to different interpretations[23]. The simplest, *vernacular*, solution consists in a direct adaptation to the natural space. In a defined valley this would mean to form a row parallel to the direction of the land, that is, along the natural path of communication. This pattern is found in many countries, for instance in the narrow valleys of Telemark and Setesdal in Norway, where the row-*tun* is the dominant type of rural settlement[24]. An *urban* valley-settlement, instead, represents a centre which gathers the surrounding space. This is achieved by introducing an axis across the valley, mostly in connection with a ford or a bridge-point. The centre thus formed is still a function of local circumstances without "cosmic" implications. When the Romans used a site of this kind, however, they usually placed their *cardo-decumanus* axes on one side of the river, reducing thus the importance of the local space (London, Paris, Cologne, Ratisbon, Turin, etc.). The Roman colonial settlement therefore represented an absolute system, albeit of natural derivation, rather than a gathering of the local landscape. This is particularly evident in Florence where the Roman axes were turned at an angle to the river and the valley. During the Middle Ages the boundary of the urban enclosure was turned back to correspond with the river. Another example of "place-free", "cosmic" orientation is the traditional east-west axis of the Christian church, which in many Mediaeval towns contradicts the dominant directions of the urban tissue.

Settlements on a plain have analogous possibilities of interpretation. Here the basic vernacular form is not the row,

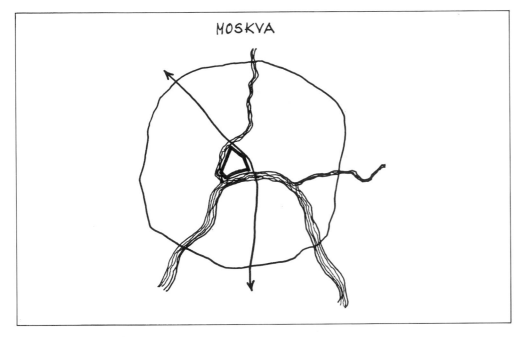

MOSKVA

but the dense cluster or the enclosure (*Rundling, Vierkanthof*). These forms express the general, directionless extension of the surrounding land. The development of an urban centre is usually combined with geometrization, such as the building or a regular, square or rectangular enclosure (Montagnana etc.), or, less frequently, a ring. When a river is present, interesting combinations of enclosure and longitudinal-transversal directions are formed. A good example is furnished by Moscow, where the triangular shape of the Kremlin is due to the interpenetration of ring, river and transverse axis. On a plain, the Roman scheme is congenial, but evidently it still represents an abstraction, as is shown by Lucca, where the system was filled in by a dense cluster of houses during the Middle Ages.

Building in an extended hilly landscape poses different problems. Here directions are neither in fact nor potentially present, and the only possible structuration consists in visualizing the tops and crests by means of concentrated or longitudinal clusters. The result is well known from Italy, where "hill-towns" are legion. In general they belong to the vernacular category, but sometimes they gain the importance of a centre, mainly due to an isolated, dominant location (Orvieto) or through vertical accentuation (Palombara). A centre is also formed when several crests meet, as is the case in Siena, where the town integrates three significant directions: north (Florence), south (Rome) and west (Grosseto, coast). When the scale increases and the hills become mountains, the settlements are usually located in the sloping mountain-side, forming a series of terraces. Good examples are furnished by Gubbio and Assisi. Terraces also represent a natural solution when an amphitheatrical bay has to be built, which moreover demands a continuous

289. *Alatri, Lazio.*
290. *Siena.*

291. *Assisi in the landscape.*
292. *Assisi from above.*

engirdling disposition of the houses. Islands and promontories are somewhat related to the tops and crests of the inland. Sperlonga is thus clustered along the crest of a promontory, whereas the Castello on the Island of Giglio rests on an isolated hillock near the top of the island. On the same island an archetypal bay-settlement is also found (Giglio Porto).

Our few remarks on the location and spatial morphology of settlements might seem trivial. Today, however, these simple structural relationships are hardly understood and still less respected. As the general identity of our places depends on such structures, they form an important part of the phenomenology of architecture. In general, all the types of settlement mentioned, represent variations on the *figure-ground* theme. We understand that "figure" here does not mean a "foreign" element which appears on a "neutral" ground, but a visualization of potentially present foci.

So far, we have mainly treated the external structure of settlements, that is, their "direct" relation to the environment. The *internal* structure is necessarily coordinated with the external relations. The urban spaces do not form an independent interior world. To allow for man's orientation and identification they have to concretize the general situation of the settlement. Obviously this cannot be done by means of visualization, and symbolization comes to play a decisive role. This implies that the aspect of character gains in importance, but a few spatial problems also have to be mentioned. Whereas the interior spaces of vernacular settlements form a continuation of the surroundings, or a simple "space within space" relationship[26], urban settlements are distinguished by a definition of spatial foci which make the citizen experience the general role of the place as a local or

regional centre. To fullfil their function, these spaces ought to contain all those "things" (buildings, monuments etc.) which make manifest the meanings gathered by the place. Thus Heidegger says: "...the things themselves *are* the places, and do not only "belong" to a place"[27]. In European towns the path structure is usually centred on the foci, making thus the whole settlement appear as a meaningful organism, where the meanings present at the centre determine the form, in interaction with the external situation. The paths so to speak illustrate how the meanings were brought inside from the "threshold" of the city gate.

Examples which illustrate the role of urban foci as gathering centres are legion. We have already mentioned the Greek *agora* and the Roman *forum*, and may add the Mediaeval markets and cathedral squares[28]. On the European continent the cathedral is preceded by an urban space which serves to unite the symbolic interior of the building with the town as a whole. The integration of outside and inside is furthermore expressed by deep embrasured portals. In England, instead, the cathedral is located within a precinct; a more conservative solution which divides space in two qualitatively different domains. The formal solution of the urban foci is particularly beautiful in Siena, where the squares of cathedral and town hall are placed on either side of the meeting point of the three paths mentioned above. A splendid answer to the problem of urban gathering is also offered by St. Mark's square in Venice, where the large *piazza* forms a meaningful transition between the dense labyrinth of the city and the glittering expanse of the sea.

The urban paths and squares are constituted by buildings which embody the meanings gathered by the city. We have

already shown that this embodiment depends upon how the buildings *stand*, *rise* and *open*, and have mentioned that their "behaviour" is usually condensed in *motifs* which characterize an urban environment as a whole. Such motifs are not applied decoration, but consist in a characteristic solution of the "critical parts" of the structure[29]. Analyzing the functions of standing, rising and opening, it follows that the critical parts are base, roof, corner and opening (window, door); that is, the "elements" which relate the building to its environment and defines how it "is" on the earth[30]. The possible solutions are obviously legion, but some primary types of motifs may be singled out.

In general a building may stand *in* the ground, *on* the ground, or *over* the ground. To be "in the ground" expresses an intimate "romantic" relationship to the "forces" of the earth. It is usually concretized by making the building grow out of the ground without a distinct base. "On the ground", instead, means that the building is set off on a base as an individual, "classical" thing between earth and sky. "Over the ground", finally, implies that the continuity of the ground is preserved; the building is placed on de-materialized stilts (*pilotis*), and seems to exist in an abstract, "cosmic" space.

There are also three basic types of rising. Either the building is vertically "open" and joins the sky in a "free" and serrate silhouette, or it is "closed" as an individual body by means of a heavy entablature or voluminous roof, or it is simply delimited by a neutral horizontal line which gives emphasis to lateral extension.

The basic types of opening depend on the conservation or dissolution of the continuity of the boundary. In any case the result is determined by the size, shape and distribution of the openings.

299. *Sacred, military and residential architecture, Ostia Antica.*

300. *Standing and rising. Old house in Rothenburg.*

301. *Standing and rising. Palazzo Comunale, Velletri.*

302. *Standing and rising. Kloster Banz, corner pavilion by Neumann.*

303. *Window in Salerno.*
304. *Window in Paris.*

305. *Window at the Upper Belvedere, Vienna by Hildebrandt.*
306. *Window at St. George in the East, London by Hawksmoor.*

It is thus possible to create a "romantic" interplay between exterior and interior by means of irregular and surprising transitions; or a clearly defined communication where inside and outside preserve their distinct identities; or an abstract, systematic integration where the two domains seem made of the same extended "substance". Among all *motifs*, the window is particularly important. It does not only express the spatial structure of the building, but also how it is related to light. And, through its proportions and detailing, it participates in the functions of standing and rising. In the window, thus, the *genius loci* is focused and "explained".

The *identity* of a place is determined by location, general spatial configuration and characterizing articulation. As a totality we experience for instance a place as "a dense cluster of enclosed stone houses in a hill side", or as "a continuous row of brightly coloured veranda houses around a small bay", or as "an ordered group of half-timbered gable houses in a valley". Location, configuration and articulation do not always contribute in the same measure to the final result. Some places get their identity from a particularly interesting location, whereas the man-made components are rather insignificant. Others, instead, may be situated in a dull landscape, but possess a well-defined configuration and a distinct character. When *all* the components seem to embody basic existential meanings, we may talk about a "strong" place[31]. The three cities analyzed above, are such strong places, although Khartoum leaves something to be desired as regards characterizing articulation. The elements, however, are there, and the "strength" of the place could easily be improved if the *genius loci* is understood and respected.

In any case a strong place presupposes

307. *Theme and variation. Dutch town.*
308. *Theme and variation. Houses at Procida, Naples.*
309. *Porch-motif. Street in Cambridge, Mass.*
310. *Massive and skeleton structure. Farm in the Po-valley.*

that there exists a meaningful correspondence between site, settlement and architectural detail. The man-made place has to know "what it wants to be" relative to the natural environment. Such a correspondence can be achieved in many different ways. We have already mentioned the vernacular "adaptation" and the urban "interpretation". The possibilities of interpretation are evidently determined by the site itself and by the historical circumstances which may both favour a certain approach of the "romantic", "cosmic" or "classical" type. Moreover an interpretation is always open to individual variations. In general settlements are therefore characterized by basic motifs which are varied according to the circumstances. *Theme and variation* is in fact a basic means of artistic concretization. The "theme" represents a general complex of meanings, and the "variations" its circumstantial realization. Such themes may be a particular type of building as well as motifs of "critical" importance. Well-known examples are the Italian *palazzo*, the French *hôtel* of the *cour d'honneur* type, and the Central European *Bürgerhaus*[32]. The *entrance* is also in most settlements a characteristic motif of "thematic" importance. American towns are thus distinguished by the varied repetition of conspicuous porches. In general "theme and variation" allows for the expression of individual identity within a system of manifest common meanings. Thus it conserves the "spirit" of the place without making it become a life-less straightjacket.

3. History

Our discussion of the identity of a place has already brought us close to the problem of constancy and change. How does a place preserve its identity under the pressure of historical forces? How can a place adapt to the changing needs of public and private life? The common *laissez faire* attitude of today implies a rejection of the first question and a blind acceptance of adaptation to change. We have tried to show, however, that human identity presupposes the identity of place, and that *stabilitas loci* therefore is a basic human need. The development of individual and social identity is a slow process, which cannot take place in a continuously changing environment. We have every reason to believe that the human alienation so common today, to a high extent is due to the scarce possibilities of orientation and identification offered by the modern environment. Piaget's researches in fact show that a mobile world would tie man to an egocentric stage of development, while a stabile and structured world frees his mental powers[33]. Our analysis of the cities of Prague, Khartoum and Rome have moreover shown that it *is* possible to preserve the *genius loci* over considerable periods of time without interfering with the needs of successive historical situations.

Let us sum up *what* ought to be preserved, before we embark up upon a discussion of the problem of change. The *genius loci* becomes manifest as location, spatial configuration and characterizing articulation. All these aspects to some extent have to be preserved, as they are the objects of man's orientation and indentification. What has to be respected are obviously their *primary* structural properties, such as the type of settlement and way of building ("massive", "skeletal" etc.) as well as characteristic motifs. Such properties are always capable of various interpretations if they are properly understood, and therefore do not hamper stylistic changes and individual creativity. If the primary structural properties are respected, the general atmosphere or *Stimmung* will not get lost. It is this *Stimmung* which first of all ties man to "his" place and strikes the visitor as a particular local quality[34]. The idea of preservation, however, also has another purpose. It implies that architectural history is understood as a collection of cultural experiences, which should not get lost but remain present as *possibilities* for human "use".

What kind of changes does history ask for? In general they may be grouped in three categories: practical changes, social changes, and cultural changes. All these changes have physical (environmental) implications. As the cultural and social changes become manifest through their physical implications, we may consider the problem of change in "functional" terms, and ask: How can the *genius loci* be preserved under the pressure of new functional demands? What happens for instance when new or larger streets become necessary? The example of Prague has taught us that a system of paths may develop during history in conformity with the structure of the natural place. We may also remind of Rome, where the breaking through of Corso Vittorio Emanuele (after 1886) fairly well respected the continuity and scale of the traditional Roman street, whereas the *sventramenti* carried out under Fascism introduced a new and "foreign" urban pattern, although the aim was to restore the "greatness" of the Imperial capital[35]. We understand, thus, that it makes sense to talk about "good" and "bad" changes.

One might object, however, that our three main examples are not suitable for illustrating the problem of change. When Prague and Rome started to feel the full impact of modern life, their old centres were already under protection, and Khartoum is still waiting for becoming a modern metropolis. But the problem of change is not basically different if

we consider a great and truly modern city such as Chicago. Even here the *genius loci* is of decisive importance, and changes have to obey to certain "rules". The infinite extension of the great plains and Lake Michigan is thus reflected in an "open", orthogonal urban structure, which is concretized in each single building. Enclosed, round or "freely" shaped buildings are "meaningless" in Chicago; the place demands a regular grid. The *genius loci* was understood by the early pioneers, and was set-into-work in the famous "Chicago-construction" which was invented by Jenney about 1880. The local tradition was carried on after 1937 by Mies van der Rohe, whose personal idiom fitted Chicago perfectly. The last and most impressive interpretation of the spirit of Chicago has been given in the 420 metres tall Sears Tower by SOM[36]. Today there is hardly any place where architects are so conscious of the need for adapting to the given environment, and this happens in a city which is among the most dynamic in the world! It would of course have been *possible* to interpret Chicago differently. The interpretation chosen, however, evidently suited the economic, social, political and cultural intentions of the pioneers. They wanted to concretize the image of an open and dynamic world of opportunities, and chose an appropriate spatial system.

This does not mean, however, that Chicago architecture may be used whenever similar intentions have to be set-into-work. Other places have a different relationship to "open" form, and have to be treated accordingly. Boston may serve as an interesting example. Until quite recently Boston appeared as a dense cluster of relatively small houses on the peninsula between the harbour and the Charles River[37]. The architectural quality was generally very high,

and the environment characterized by significant local motifs. During the last decade large parts of the urban tissue have been erased, and scattered "super-buildings" erected instead. The development culminated with the John Hancock Tower by I.M. Pei, which completely destroys the scale of a major urban focus, Copley Square[38]. As a result, Boston today appears a hybrid city; the old remains, such as Beacon Hill, make the new buildings look inhuman and ridiculous, and the new structure have a crushing effect on the old environment, not only because of the scale, but because of their total lack of architectural character. Thus the place has lost its meaningful relationship to earth and sky.

Our examples show that economic, social, political and cultural intentions have to be concretized in a way which respects the *genius loci*. If not, the place loses its identity. In Boston the *genius loci* was for a long time understood; recently, however, a way of building has been introduced which is foreign to the place, and which deprives man of the satisfaction of one of his most fundamental needs: a meaningful environment. Whereas Chicago possesses the capacity for absorbing this kind of buildings, Boston does not. Thus we learn that cities have to be treated as *individual places*, rather than abstract spaces where the "blind" forces of economy and politics may have free play[39]. To respect the *genius loci* does not mean to copy old models. It means to determine the identity of the place and to interpret it in ever new ways. Only then we may talk about a *living tradition* which makes change meaningful by relating it to a set of locally founded parametres. We may again remind of Alfred North Whitehead's dictum: "The art of progress is to preserve order amid change, and change

amid order"[40]. A living tradition serves life because it satisfies these words. It does not understand "freedom" as an arbitrary play, but as creative participation.

In our context "creative participation" means two things: firstly the realization of a *private* "inside" which concretizes the identity of the individual by gathering the meanings which constitute his personal existential content, and secondly the creation of a *public* "outside" which gathers the institutions of communal life and makes the meanings (values) manifest on which this life is based. The private domain is the home of man, in the narrower sense of the word. It is personal, but not singular. Personal "foothold" implies an understanding of *a shared environment* (a common place), and therefore has to be concretized as a *variation on a theme*. The theme consists in a typical spatial relationship between inside and outside, and in certain locally meaningful motifs. In the Nordic countries, for instance, the house has to give man physical protection by being enclosed. At the same time he wants it to be *symbolically open* to bring nature near. Thus we find, for instance, a characteristic tendency to use "natural" materials inside[41]. In the desert the house is enclosed both in a pratical and a symbolic sense; it represents a different "paradisical" world which forms a complement to the outside. In the "classical" countries a favourable climate and a trustworthy, imageable nature makes the outside become an inside; the boundary between private and public domains is weakened, and if it is maintained, it is to make the inside a place of representation rather than a home.

In general the conception of the private inside becomes manifest in the "threshold" or boundary which separates it from *and* unifies it with the outside. At

314. *Norwegian cottage, Telemark.*
315. *African house from Sudan.*

316. *Street in old Naples.*
317. *Street "of agreement" in Einbeck, Germany.*
318. *From the agora of Priene.*

the same time the boundary gives the public outside its particular presence. Thus Louis Kahn says: "The street is a room of agreement. The street is dedicate by each house owner to the city..."[42]. But the public outside is something more than an "agreement" of individual homes. The agreement it represents is focused in public buildings which concretize the shared understanding which makes communal life possible and meaningful. These public buildings ought to appear as particularly complete and articulate variations on the themes which are already intoned in the single home. This was the case in the Greek *polis*, where the public buildings *expose* those meaningful forms which in a more modest way were used inside the dwellings (such as the anthropomorphous column), and especially in the Mediaeval town where the exteriors of houses, churches and town halls are variations on themes which express an integrated form of life. To fullfil its purpose, the public domain obviously has to be spatially integrated; scattered institutions do not form any true urban place.

We have introduced the concept of "theme and variation" as an answer to the problem of constancy and change. The concept does not contain anything new, it only expresses in a clearer way what it means to respect the *genius loci*. A theme is a symbolic form which embodies existential meanings. As such it has to be circumstantial *and* general. It has to concretize the local circumstances, but at the same time it should present these as a particular manifestation of a general universe of meanings. The relationship between the local and the general has been discussed in terms of "romantic", "cosmic" and "classical" environments. The "romantic", "cosmic" and "classical" modes grasp the dominant character of a particular place, at the same time as

they are general categories of understanding, which directs attention towards certain types of meanings. The three categories cover objective environmental properties as well as human attitudes, and therefore grasp the correspondence (*Übereinstimmung*) which ought to form the basis of our being-in-the-world. It helps our understanding to relate the architectural themes to these categories, although it has to be repeated that any concrete situation comprises elements from all of them. The categories have been introduced because human identity consists in a particular kind of correspondence.

As one gets to know different countries; talking with people, eating with people, feeling with people, reading their literature, listening to their music and using their places, one beings to realize that the correspondence of man and place has not changed much throughout history[43]. The local human attitude is surprisingly constant, and we must agree with Hegel when he says that it determines the people's "place in world history". We can therefore repeat that the basic existential contents are not produced by changing economical, social and political conditions. The existential contents have deeper roots, and the changing conditions only ask for ever new interpretations. The crucial question therefore is: "How is it possible to remain an Italian, a Russian, or a German under *this* regime?" Regimes come and go, the place persists, and with it a particular kind of human identity. When we have realized this fact, we should start to improve the world by taking care of our places, rather than by abstract planning and anonymous building[44]. Thus we may leave utopia behind and return to the things of our everyday life-world.

Creative participation means to concretize the basic meanings under ever new historical circumstances. Participation, however, can only be obtained "by great labor"[45]. The "threshold" which is the symbol of participation, is in fact "turned to stone" by "pain". Participation presupposes *sympathy* with things, to repeat the word of Goethe, and sympathy necessarily implies suffering. In our context sympathy with things means that we *learn to see*. We have to be able to "see" the meanings of the things that surround us; be they natural or man-made. Things always tell several stories; they tell about their own making, they tell about the historical circumstances under which they were made, and if they are real things, they also reveal truth. The ability of a thing to reveal truth depends upon *how* it is made, and the next thing to learn is therefore *making*. Seeing and making are united in inspiration and concretization. Thus Louis Kahn said: "Inspiration is the moment of possibility when what to do meets the means of doing it"[46]. Seing and making constitute the basis of *dwelling*.

The results of creative participation constitute man's existential foothold, his *culture*. They make manifest what he has managed to make out of his existence. Some of the results illuminate a wider range of phenomena than others, and deserve the name "work of art". In the work of art man *praises existence*. In his *Ninth Elegy* and his *Sonnets to Orpheus*, Rilke develops the image of man as a praising singer. We remember his question: "Are we perhaps *here* to say: house, bridge, fountain, gate, jug, fruit tree, window, at best: column, tower...", and hear his answer:

"Praise to the Angel our world, not the untellable:
you can't impress *him* with grand emotion. In the cosmos
where he so powerfully feels, you're only a newcomer.

Then show his some simple thing,
grown up through generations
till it became ours, and lives near our
hands and in our eyes.
Tell him of things and he'll stand
astonished, as you stood
beside the rope-maker in Rome, or with
the Nile potter.
Show his how joyful a thing can be,
how innocent and ours,
how even lamenting sorrow can take
purely its own form,
serve as a thing, or die as a thing – and
in ecstacy
escape beyond the violin. And these
things,
that live only in passing, understand
that you praise them;
fugitive, they look to us, the most
fugitive, for rescue.
They want us entirely to transform them
in our invisible hearts
into – oh, infinitely – into us! Who-
ever we finally are"[47].

321. *Fountain.*
322. *Gate.*

323. *Fruit-tree.*
324. *Window.*

325. *Column.*
326. *Tower.*

327. *Visual chaos, Oslo.*
328. *Space between two epochs. Galleria Vittorio Emanuele, Milan by Mengoni.*
329. *Character between two epochs. Castel Béranger, Paris by Guimard.*
330. *Devaluation of symbols. Palazzo di Giustizia, Rome by Calderini.*

1. The Loss of Place

After the second world war most places have been subjected to profound changes. The qualities which traditionally distinguished human settlements have been corrupted or have got irreparably lost. Reconstructed or new towns also look very different from the places of the past. Before we consider the reasons for this fundamental change, it is necessary to give it a more precise definition in structural terms. Again it is useful to employ our concepts of "space" and "character", and relate them to the more general categories of natural and man-made place.

Spatially the new settlements do not anymore possess enclosure and density. They usually consist of buildings "freely" placed within a park-like space. Streets and squares in the traditional sense are no longer found, and the general result is a scattered assembly of units. This implies that a distinct figure-ground relationship no more exists; the continuity of the landscape is interrupted and the buildings do not form clusters or groups. Although a general order may be present, particularly when the settlement is seen from an airplane, it usually does not bring about any sense of place. The changes done to already existing towns have analogous effects. The urban tissue is "opened up", the continuity of the urban "walls" is interrupted, and the coherence of the urban spaces damaged. As a consequence, nodes, paths and districts lose their identity, and the town as a whole its imageability. Together with the loss of the traditional urban structure, the landscape is deprived of its meaning as comprehensive extension, and reduced to rests within the complex network of man-made elements.

The *character* of the present day environment is usually distinguished by monotony. If any variety is found, it is

331. *Monotony. New suburb in Moscow.*

332. *Visual chaos, USA.*

333. *The "open" city. Federal Center, Chicago by Mies van der Rohe.*

usually due to elements left over from the past. The "presence" of the majority of new buildings is very weak. Very often "curtain-walls" are used which have an unsubstantial and abstract character, or rather, a lack of character. Lack of character implies poverty of stimuli. The modern environment in fact offers very little of the surprises and discoveries which make the experience of old towns so facinating. When attempts to break the general monotony are made, they mostly appear as arbitrary fancies.

In general, the symptoms indicate a *loss of place*. Lost is the settlement as a place in nature, lost are the urban foci as places for common living, lost is the building as a meaningful sub-place where man may simultaneously experience individuality and belonging. Lost is also the relationship to earth and sky. Most modern buildings exist in a "nowhere"; they are not related to a landscape and not to a coherent, urban whole, but live their abstract life in a kind of mathematical-technological space which hardly distinguishes between up and down. The same feeling of "nowhere" is also encountered in the interiors of the dwellings. A neutral, flat surface has substituted the articulate ceilings of the past, and the window is reduced to a standard device which lets in a measurable quantity of air and light. In most modern rooms it is meaningless to ask: "What slice of sun does your building have?", that is: "what range of moods does the light offer from morning to night, from day to day, from season to season, and all through the years?"[1]. In general, all *qualities* are lost, and we may indeed talk about an "environmental crisis".

It has often been pointed out that the modern environment makes human orientation difficult. The work of Kevin Lynch evidently took this deficiency as

334. The "Green City" by Le Corbusier.
335. Pavillon de l'esprit nouveau by Le Corbusier (1925), rebuilt in Bologna 1977.

its point of departure, and he implies that poor imageability may cause emotional insecurity and fear[2]. The effects of scarce possibilities of identification, however, have hardly been the subject of direct study. From psychological literature we know that a general poverty of stimuli may cause passivity and reduced intellectual capacity[3], and we may also infer that human identity in general depends on growing up in a "characteristic" environment[4]. The environmental crisis therefore implies a *human* crisis. Evidently the environmental problem has to be met with intelligence and efficiency. In our opinion this can only be done on the basis of an understanding of the concept of place. "Planning" does not help much as long as the concrete, qualitative nature of places is ignored. How, then, may a theory of place help us to solve our actual problems? Before we give some suggestions for the answers to this question, we have, however, to say a few words about the reasons for the environmental crisis.

Paradoxically, the present situation is a result of a wish for making man's environment better. The open, "green city" thus represented a reaction against the inhuman conditions in the industrial cities of nineteenth century Europe, and modern architecture in general took the need for better dwellings as its point of departure[5]. Le Corbusier wrote: "Man dwells badly, that is the deep and real reason for the upheavals of our time"[6], and at the Exposition Internationale des Arts Décoratifs in Paris 1925, he showed a prototype apartment which he called the *Pavillon de l'esprit nouveau*. To demonstrate the "spirit" of the modern age, he thus made a dwelling for the common man. Le Corbusier's point of view is clearly indicated in *Vers une Architecture* (1923). Here he tells us that "we are to be pitied for living in

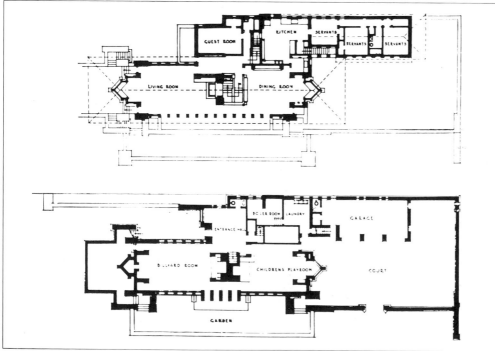

unworthy houses, since they ruin our health and our morale"[7]. The new spirit therefore aimed at something more than the satisfaction of mere physical needs. Evidently it implied a new way of life which should make man "normal" again, in the sense of allowing him to follow "the organic development of his existence"[8]. At the root of the modern movement, as defined by Le Corbusier, was the wish to help alienated modern man to regain a true and meaningful existence. To achieve this he needed "freedom" as well as "identity". "Freedom" meant primarily liberation from the absolutist systems of the Baroque age and their successors, that is, a new right to choose and participate. "Identity" meant to bring man back to what is original and essential. The modern movement in fact used the slogan *Neue Sachlichkeit*, which ought to be translated "back to things" rather than "new rationalism".

The work of the first of modern pioneers, Frank Lloyd Wright, was from the very beginning conditioned by a concrete "hunger for reality", and at 11 he was sent to a Wisconsin farm "to learn how to really work"[9]. As a result, his approach to the natural phenomena did not consist in the abstract observation and analysis common in Europe, but in the direct experience of archetypal, meaningful "forces". Thus he said: "It comforted me to see the fire burning deep in the solid masonry of the house itself"[10], and accordingly he developed his plans around a large chimney-stack, to make the fire-place the expressive core of the dwelling. His use of natural materials must also be understood as the manifestation of a wish for a return to the concrete phenomena, that is, for a "deeper sense of reality"[11]. Wright was also the first to give an answer to the demand for "freedom". Traditionally the human dwelling had

been a refuge for the individual and the family. Wright wanted rootedness *and* freedom, and thus he destroyed the traditional "box" and created a new interaction between inside and outside by means of continuous walls which direct and unify space. The concept of inside is thereby changed from a refuge to a fixed point in space, from which man could experience a new sense of freedom and participation. This point is marked by the great fireplace with its vertical chimney. Hence man no longer places himself at the center of the world as was the case in Versailles. Rather we find at the centre an element which symbolizes the forces and order of nature. A remainder evidently, that the modern world should not negate the basic meanings of existence.

The work of Wright made a profound impression on the European pioneers after its publication in Germany in 1910. Evidently they recognized that Wright had managed to define the concrete means which were needed to give man a new dwelling. It is important in this context also to mention his idea of an "architecture of democracy". Before, architecture was determined from "above", and the dwelling only reflected the meaningful forms developed in connection with church and palace. Modern architecture, on the contrary, takes the dwelling as its point of departure, and all other building tasks are considered "extensions" of the dwelling, to use the term of Le Corbusier[12]. The traditional order of building tasks is thereby reversed. This means that architecture is no longer based on dogma and authority, but ought to grow out of daily life, as an expression of man's understanding of nature, of other men and of himself. The "higher" building tasks thus become a result rather than a condition, and they represent something man must conquer in his own life. The *esprit*

nouveau therefore should free man from the "systems", and conquer the split of thought and feeling which was a characteristic product of bourgeois society[13].

Why, then, did the modern movement lead to the loss of place rather than a reconquest? As far as we can see, the main reasons are two, and both imply an insufficient understanding of the concept of place. They are moreover related to the dimensions of "space" and "character" and thus confirm the validity of our approach. The first reason has to do with the crisis as an *urban* problem. The loss of place is first of all felt on the urban level, and is, as we have seen, connected with a loss of the spatial structures which secure the identity of a settlement. Instead of being an urban place, the modern settlement is conceived as a "blown-up house", of the type developed by the pioneers of modern architecture: Frank Lloyd Wright, Le Corbusier, and Mies van der Rohe. The plan of the modern house was defined as "open", and the space as a "flowing" continuum which hardly distinguished between outside and inside. Such a space may be appropriate for a sub-urban one-family house (as was the ideal of Wright), but it is questionable whether it suits an urban situation. In the city a clear distinction between private and public domains is necessary, and space cannot "flow" freely. This problem was, however, partly understood by the pioneers; the urban houses of Le Corbusier constitute true "insides" and Mies van der Rohe already in 1934 suggested the use of enclosed "court houses" for the city[14]. When we talk about the modern settlement as a "blown-up house", we rather have in mind the fact that *quarters* and *cities* are conceived as large open plans. In the urban projects of the 'twenties and 'thirties, and in many neighbourhoods which are built today,

true urban "insides" are lacking; the space is freely flowing between slab-like buildings which resemble the freestanding walls of an "open" plan, such as the plan of the Barcelona-pavilion by Mies van der Rohe (1929). Spatially, the modern city is therefore based on a *confusion of scales*; a pattern which might be valid on one level is blindly transferred to another. This unfortunate "solution" to the problem of the settlement became possible because the concept of "milieu" was at the outset of the modern movement only understood in physical terms, that is, as a mere need for "air, light and green"[15].

The second reason has to do with the idea of an *international style*[16]. In the 'twenties it was maintained that modern architecture should not be local or regional, but follow the same principles everywhere. It is characteristic that the first volume in the series of *Bauhausbücher* was called *Internationale Architektur*. Although Gropius reacted against the world "style", he thus embraced the idea of internationalism. Thus he said: ..."The forms of the New Architecture differ fundamentally... from those of the old, they are... simply the inevitable, logical product of the intellectual, social and technical conditions of our age"[17]. This does not mean, however, that modern architecture was conceived as a mere practical product; it also ought to give "aesthetic satisfaction to the human soul"[18]. This satisfaction ought to be achieved by substituting a "welter of ornament" with simple, mass-produced forms. The result was what Venturi appropriately has called an "architecture of exclusion". This does not mean, however, that the buildings of the European pioneers were aesthetically poor, or "characterless", in an absolute sense. On the contrary, some of them, such as Le Corbusier's Villa Savoye (1928-31) and Mies van der Rohe's Tugendhat House (1930), are true masterpieces which in a convincing way concretize a new way of life. Although they lack the "substance" and presence of many old buildings, their volumetric composition and structural integrity fully satisfy modern man's demand for freedom and identity. Moreover they undoubtedly represent a reconquest of essential meanings and means, and hence a new *Sachlichkeit*, in the true sense of the word. But something strange happens when the ascetic character of early modernism is transferred to the *urban* level. What was a subtle interplay of forms, which (almost) confirms Mies' thesis that "less is more", becomes sterile monotony[19]. The essence of settlement consists in *gathering*, and gathering means that different meanings are brought together. The architecture of exclusion mainly told us that the modern world is "open"; a statement which in a certain sense is anti-urban. Openness cannot be gathered. Openness means departure, gathering means return.

It is somewhat unfair, however, to blame the modern movement for shortcomings which only belonged to a certain phase of its development. The modern movement did not come to an end with the images of a green city and an international architecture. Already in 1944 the spokesman of the movement, S. Giedion, put forward the demand for a "new monumentality" and said: "Monumentality springs from the eternal need of people to create symbols for their activities and for their fate or destiny, for their religious belief and for their social convinctions"[20]. And in 1951 a CIAM conference discussed the *Core of the City*, that is, the problem of introducing in the open tissue of the modern settlement a gathering focus. Again we may refer to Giedion: "Contemporary interest in the core is part of

a general humanizing process; of a return to the human scale and the assertion of the rights of the individual..."[21]. Finally, in 1954, Giedion wrote an essay with the title "On the New Regionalism" where he asked for a new respect for the "way of life", which ought to be studied with "reverence" before designing a project. "The new regionalism has as its motivating force a respect for individuality and a desire to satisfy the emotional and material needs of each area"[22]. We understand thus, that the leaders of the modern movement already 20-30 years ago foresaw some of the most important problems we are facing now. Those who got stuck with the early images of a green city and standardized form, were the epigones and vulgarizers of modern architecture.

2. The Recovery of Place

The critics of the modern movement usually take the general discontent with our present environment as their point of departure, and maintain that modern architecture has not been able to solve the problem. Furthermore they often criticize the architects for carrying out any commission without taking into consideration the consequences of their actions for society and the anonimous "user". Thus the social psychologist Alfred Lorenzer writes: "The architect as a mere technical aid to the dominant powers, corresponds to the ideal of consequent functionalists. The *sacrificium intellectus* of these architects is architecture"[23]. Whereas we have taken the general criticism very seriously, and asked whether the modern movement really failed in giving man a new dwelling, the statement of Lorenzer sounds rather surprising to those who have participated actively in the propagation of modern architecture. It is certainly possible to find cases when protagonists of the modern movement

served as "aids" to the dominant powers, but the fact that many of them had to leave their countries or withdraw from active professional life because of their artistic creed, is certainly more significant. Thus Giedion could write: "Architecture has long ceased to be the concern of passive and businesslike specialists who built precisely what their clients demanded. It has gained the courage to deal with life..."[24]. The criticism of Lorenzer therefore only holds true for the work of certain imitators who did not really understand the aims of the modern movement, and his criticism obviously stems from an insufficient comprehension of the concept of "functionalism". We have demonstrated that the point of departure of the modern movement was profoundly meaningful and that its development showed an ever more complete understanding of the environmental problem. A *constructive* criticism on this basis is given by Robert Venturi in his remarkable book *"Complexity and Contradiction in Architecture"*, which advocates a "both-and" rather than an "either-or" approach[25].

The basic aim of the second phase of modern architecture is to give buildings and places individuality, with regard to space and character. This means to take the circumstantial conditions of locality and building task into consideration, rather than basing the design upon general types and principles. The new approach became manifest in the works of Alvar Aalto already before the second world war. In general Aalto wants to adapt the spatial structure of his buildings as well as the surrounding space, and thus he reintroduces topological forms which were hardly admitted by early functionalism. His approach was shown in a programmatic way in the Finnish pavilion at the World's Fair in New York 1939, and found a con-

vincing realization in his MIT Senior Dormitory in Cambridge, Mass. (1947-48). The undulating wall of this building concretizes the general modern idea of "freedom", at the same time as it represents an adaptation to the spatial circumstances. Aalto also aimed at giving his architecture an outspoken local character. In works such as Villa Mairea (1938-39) and the town-hall in Säynätsalo (1945-52), the Finnish *genius loci* is strongly present[26]. Mairea may in fact be considered the first manifestation of the new "regional" approach. Again, thus, the development of modern architecture took the dwelling as its point of departure. The works of Aalto are eminently "romantic", and illustrate how this attitude was able to free modern architecture from the "cosmic" abstractions of early European modernism. Thus Aalto satisfies Wright's "hunger for reality".

A hunger for reality was also felt by Le Corbusier, although he, as a child of European civilization, did not have that direct contact with the concrete phenomena which was normal in the "new world" of America, or in countries such as Finland, where popular traditions and a more "natural" way of life had survived. Le Corbusier therefore needed a long and "patient search" (to use his own words), before he could give buildings true presence and character. In his *Unité d'Habitation* in Marseilles (1947-52), however, a new plastic force becomes manifest. The slender *pilotis* of the thirties have become massive and powerful, and the abstract outer skin has been replaced by a *brise-soleil* which characterizes the building as a sculptural body. "A new, mid-twentieth-century image of the embattled human presence in the world"[27], is thus concretized. The great turning point, however, came with the church of Ronchamp (1953-55). Here the psychological dimension of

196

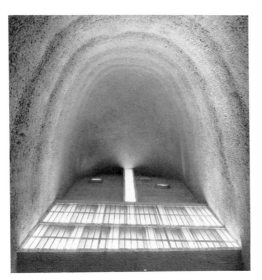

341. *Ste. Marie du Haut, Ronchamp by Le Corbusier, detail.*
342. *Ste. Marie du Haut, Ronchamp by Le Corbusier, interior detail.*
343. *Ste. Marie du Haut, Ronchamp by Le Corbusier.*

architecture returns with full force. Le Corbusier himself said that he wanted to create "a vessel of intense concentration and meditation"[28]. In fact the building has become a true centre of meaning and a "gathering force", as Vincent Scully said with fine intuitive understanding[29]. Le Corbusier recognized also at an early date the gathering nature of the urban settlement, and indicated the idea of a "core" which comprises the important institutions of the community (St. Dié 1945). His search in this direction culminated with the Capitol of Chandigarh in India (1951-56).

A third decisive contribution to the recovery of architecture as the making of places, must be mentioned. The work of Louis Kahn appeared as something of a revelation at a moment of crisis when many architects were losing their self-confidence and faith in architecture. Kahn's approach is defined in his dictum: "What does the building want to be?" In his projects he gives answers to this question in terms of space and character. Suddenly everything is there again: open and closed spaces, clusters and groups, symmetry and asymmetry, node and path; and above all: the wall as a "threshold" between interior and exterior. In the walls of Kahn, past and present are united, and thus he said: "I thought of wrapping ruins around buildings"[30]. First of all, however, the walls of Kahn are there to receive light, "the giver of all presences"[30]. No wonder that Vincent Scully wrote: "The impression becomes inescapable that in Kahn, as once in Wright, architecture began a-new"[12].

What then is the message of Louis Kahn?

In numerous talks he defined his position, using a very personal, poetical way of expression. At a closer scrutiny, however, a coherent philosophy of architecture emerges. First of all Kahn

344. *Unitarian Church in Rochester, N.Y. by Louis Kahn.*
345. *Rochester, interior.*
346. *Richards Medical Research Building, Philadelphia by Louis Kahn, detail.*

understood architecture in terms of place. A "room" is for him a place with its particular character, its "spiritual aura", and a building is a "society of rooms". The street is "a room of agreement", and the city "an assembly of places vested with the care to uphold the sense of a way of life"[33]. The character of places is both determined by their spatial properties and by the way they receive light. Thus he said: "The sun was not aware of its wonder before it struck the side of a building", and: "Of the elements of a room the window is the most marvelous"[34]. Here he comes very close to Heidegger, who describes a Greek temple saying: "The luster and gleam of the stone, though itself apparently glowing only by the grace of the sun, yet first brings to light the light of the day, the breadth of the sky, the darkness of the night"[35]. And Kahn even understands the concept of "setting-into-work" when he says that places "are *put into being* by inspired technology"[36]. Of particular importance in the work of Kahn is in fact the conception of architecture as *built order*. "Form is not simply function, but a conceived order; thus a being..."[37]. In the late works of Le Corbusier form became presence, but it as still conceived in "sculptural" terms. Kahn, instead, returnerd to "building" and thereby recovered a sense of truth which had for long been forgotten. His works are real things which make us aware of our existence between earth and sky.

Common to Le Corbusier and Kahn is a "classical" attitude. Both understand architecture as an embodiment of characters which are simultaneously human and natural, and their buildings give these characters material presence. Although Kahn's works are rooted in concrete phenomena, they tend towards a certain "formalism". The spatial layout starts to live its own life, and the articulation becomes a function of symmetry rather than "light". This danger is however counteracted most efficiently by the built substance.

In various ways the "third generation" of modern architects haven taken up and developed the intentions of the pioneers[38]. During the last two decades a series of significant works have been made which promise a more complete recovery of place. This does not mean, however, that the present situation is clear. The development of modern architecture makes many choices possible, and the tendency to understand things in a formalistic rather than an existential sense, is always present. In the Nordic countries, thus, the "romantic" approach of Aalto may easily degenerate into a superficial sentimental play with "anti-classical" forms. This tendency is in fact strongly felt, especially in Sweden where contact with nature has been reduced to nostalgia. In the "classical" South, on the countrary, the danger of mistaking "order" for concrete reality is most typical. The architecture of the Fascist epoch was based on this mistake, and it reappears in the strangely abstract works of Aldo Rossi and his followers which "stand frozen in surreal timelessness"[39]. Rossi calls his architecture "rational", a term which may be appropriate if it means a complete absence of live character. Rossi's conception of "typology" is certainly important, but it remains sterile as long as the local circumstances are left out. Another characteristic danger consists in mistaking character for empty "rhetoric" gestures. This tendency has been particularly strong in the United States, where architecture has become a means to demonstrate the "power" of firms and institutions. A modern "historicism" results, where those forms which were created to give man a sense of freedom and identity, are reduced to mere clichées. Whereas nineteenth century historicism should give man a "cultural alibi", modern historicism aims at proving that he is "up to date"[40].

Where then, do we find a creative interpretation of the actual situation? Where do we find an architecture which avoids the dangers mentioned above, and represents a true contribution to the solution of the environmental crisis? One of the first architects who approached the problem in a simple and human way was the Dane Jörn Utzon, who was immediately recognized by Giedion as a protagonist of the new phase of modern architecture[41]. In his residential projects, Kingo (1956), Birkehöj (1960), and Fredensborg (1962), Utzon created unified settlements which possess figural character in relation to the landscape, and a strong sense of place as a meaningful, social "inside". Moreover they have an outspoken local character and recover the traditional Danish value of cultivated intimacy. Utzon has also proved himself capable of creative adaptation to other environmental characters in his projects for the Sydney Opera House (1957) and the Theatre in Zurich (1964). His works are always "built", and possess the quality of true "things". In connection with the residential projects of Utzon, it is natural to mention the widely published Siedlung Halen near Berne by the Swiss group of architects, Atelier 5 (1961). Here we also find a strong figural character, and a most convincing identity of place. Siedlung Halen demonstrates that it is still possible to house people in dense settlements which conserve the integrity of the landscape, even in a country where land is very scarce.

Among the works of the third generation, there is one which treats the problems of place and local character in a particularly interesting way. We refer to the Finnish Students' Union Building

at Otaniemi by Reima Pietilä (1965-67). With his "Dipoli" Pietilä wanted to express "the dream of the people of the forest"[42]. To gain his end he used a new kind of topological space which visualizes the structure of the Finnish landscape, and the choice of materials and forms gives the intention a most convincing presence. In general, Dipoli represents a culmination of the "romantic" approach to architecture, and it is certainly not a "model" to be imitated everywhere. The approach of Pietilä however is universally valid, and makes us eager to see other analogous but cirumstantially different solutions. Such works actually exist. The metal-and-glass buildings of James Stirling are for instance eminently English and seem to embody "the dream of the people of the factory". In the houses of MLTW (Moore, Lyndon, Thurnbull, Whitaker), the American *genius* has found a new convincing concretization. The four architects have defined their approach with these words: "The dreams which accompany all human actions should be nurtured by the places in which people live"[43]. We may in this context also mention a more particular work, Ricardo Bofill's pyramid-monument on the border between Catalonia and France. Here the pointed shapes of the surrounding mountains are "gathered" and condensed by man-made geometry, whereas the crowning "temple" recalls a decisive moment in the history of Catalonia. A most convincing synthesis of general, local and temporal factors is thus created.

Our brief survey of the aims of Aalto, Kahn, the later Le Corbusier, and some exponents of the third generation, shows that the means for a solution of the environmental crisis exist. It has already been demonstrated, and in most convincing ways, how we may create places which serve the complexities and contra-

349. *Local character. Dipoli, Otaniemi, Finland by Reima Pietilä.*
350. *Local adaptation. Sea Ranch, Gualala, California by MLTW.*

dictions of contemporary life. When the examples still remain scattered and quantitatively scarce, it is both because of a general social inertia and because of vested interests which do not accept improvements before they "sell". A reason is also, however, the lack of a clear understanding of the environmental problem. It is our conviction that such an understanding only is possible on the basis of a *theory of place*. As particularly valuable contributions to the development of such a theory, we have mentioned the writings of Lynch and Venturi. A theory of place does not only integrate the different contributions, offering a comprehensive conception of the relationship between man and his environment, but it also shows that the history of modern architecture has a direction and a goal: architecture as the recovery of place. Thus the "new tradition" advocated by Giedion becomes meaningful. Moreover the concept of place unites modern architecture with the past. "Both above and below the surface of this century there is a new demand for continuity. It has again become apparent that human life is not limited to the period of a single life-span"[44].

When we see architecture from this point of view, we gain understanding and a direction for our work. This direction is not dictated by politics or science, but is existentially rooted in our everyday lifeworld. Its aim is to free us from abstractions and alienation, and bring us back to things. But theory is not enough to gain this end. It also presupposes that our senses and our imagination are educated. This was also understood by Giedion who concluded his book *Architecture, you and me*, with a chapter on "The demand for Imagination"[45]. Today man is mainly educated in pseudo-analytic thinking, and his knowledge consists of so-called "facts". His life, however, is becoming ever more meaningless, and ever more he understands that his "merits" do not count if he is not able to "dwell poetically". "Education through Art" is therefore more needed than ever before, and the work of art which above all ought to serve as the basis for our education, is the *place* which gives us our identity. Only when understanding our place, we may be able to participate creatively and contribute to its history.

NOTE

I
PLACE?

1. R.M. Rilke, *The Duino Elegies*, IX Elegy. New York 1972. (first German edition 1922.)

2. The concept "everyday life-world" was introduced by Husserl in *The Crisis of European Sciences and Transcendental Phenomenology*, 1936.

3. Heidegger, *Bauen Wohnen Denken*; Bollnow, *Mensch und Raum*; Merleau-Ponty, *Phenomenology of Perception*; Bachelard, *Poetics of Space*, also L. Kruse, *Räumliche Umwelt*, Berlin 1974.

4. Heidegger: Language, in *Poetry, Language, Thought*, edited by Albert Hofstadter. New York 1971.

5. *Ein Winterabend*
Wenn der Schnee ans Fenster fällt,
Lang die Abendglocke läutet,
Vielen ist der Tisch bereitet
Und das Haus ist wohlbestellt.

Mancher auf der Wanderschaft
Kommt ans Tor auf dunklen Pfaden.
Golden blüht der Baum der Gnaden
Aus der Erde kühlem Saft.

Wanderer tritt still herein;
Schmerz versteinerte die Schwelle.
Da erglänzt in reiner Helle
Auf dem Tische Brot und Wein.

6. Heidegger: op. cit. p. 199.

7. op. cit. p. 204. *Saggi e discorsi*, Milano, Mursia 1976, p. 125.

8. C. Norberg-Schulz, *Intentions in Architecture*, Oslo and London 1963. Chapter on "Symbolization".

9. See for instance J. Appleton, *The Experience of Landscape*. London 1975.

10. Heidegger, op. cit. p. 149.

11. op. cit. pp. 97, 99.

12. Heidegger, *Hebel der Hausfreund*. Pfullingen 1957, p. 13.

13. op. cit. p. 13.

14. Heidegger, *Poetry...* pp. 181-182.

15. Norberg-Schulz, *Existence, Space and Architecture*, London and New York 1971, where the concept "existential space" is used.

16. Heidegger points out the relationship between the words *gegen* (against, opposite) and *Gegend* (environment, locality).

17. This has been done by some writers such as K. Graf von Dürckheim, E. Straus and O.F. Bollnow.

18. We may compare with Alberti's distinction between "beauty" and "ornament".

19. Norberg-Schulz, *Existence...* pp. 12ff.

20. S. Giedion, *The Eternal Present: The Beginnings of Architecture*. London 1964.

21. K. Lynch, *The Image of the City*. Cambridge, Mass. 1960.

22. P. Portoghesi, *Le inibizioni dell'architettura moderna*. Bari 1975, pp. 88ff.

23. Heidegger, op. cit. p. 154.

24. Norberg-Schulz, op. cit. p. 18.

25. Heidegger, op. cit. p. 154. "Presence is the old word for being".

26. O.F. Bollnow, *Das Wesen der Stimmungen*. Frankfurt a.M. 1956.

27. R. Venturi, *Complexity and Contradiction in Architecture*. New York 1967, p. 88.

28. Venturi, op. cit. p. 89.

29. Heidegger, Die Frage nach der Technik, in *Vorträge und Aufsätze*, Pfullingen 1954, p. 12.

30. Norberg-Schulz, op. cit. p. 27.

31. op. cit. p. 32.

32. D. Frey, *Grundlegung zu einer vergleichenden Kunstwissenschaft*. Vienna and Innsbruck 1949.

33. Norberg-Schulz, *Intentions...*

34. Heidegger, *Poetry...* p. 152.

35. W.J. Richardson, *Heidegger. Through Phenomenology to Thought*. The Hague 1974, p. 585.

36. For the concept of "capacity" see Norberg-Schulz, *Intentions...*

37. Venturi, op. cit.

38. *Paulys Realencyclopedie der Classischen Altertumswissenschaft*. VII, 1, col. 1155ff.

39. Norberg-Schulz, *Meaning in Western Architecture*, London and New York 1975, pp. 10ff.

40. Goethe, *Italienische Reise*, 8. October 1786.

41. L. Durrell, *Spirit of Place*. London 1969, p. 156.

42. See M.M. Webber, *Explorations into Urban Structure*. Philadelphia 1963, who talks about "non-place urban realm".

43. Cf. Norberg-Schulz, *Intentions...* where the concepts "cognitive orientation" and "cathectic orientation" are used.

44. Lynch, op. cit. p. 4.

45. op. cit. p. 7.

46. op. cit. p. 125.

47. op. cit. p. 9.

48. For a detailed discussion, see Norberg-Schulz, *Existence...*

49. A. Rapoport, *Australian Aborigines and the Definition of Place*, in P. Oliver (ed.), *Shelter, Sign & Symbol*. London 1975.

50. Seltsam, im Nebel zu wandern!
Einsam ist jeder Busch und Stein,
Kein Baum sieht den andern,
jeder ist allein...

51. Bollnow, *Stimmungen*, p. 39.

52. Norberg-Schulz, *Intentions*, pp. 41ff.

53. Heidegger, *Poetry...* p. 181. "We are the be-thinged", the conditioned ones.

54. Heidegger, Building Dwelling Thinking, in *Poetry...* pp. 146ff.

55. op. cit. p. 147.

56. Norberg-Schulz, *Intentions...* pp. 61ff., 68.

57. op. cit. pp. 168ff.

58. Heidegger, op. cit. p. 218.

59. S. Langer, *Feeling and Form*. New York 1953.

60. Gen. 4.12.

II
NATURAL PLACE

1. The phenomenology of myths has still to be written.

2. H. and H.A. Frankfort, J.A. Wilson, T. Jacobsen, *Before Philosophy*. Harmondsworth 1949, p. 12. Also Norberg-Schulz, *Meaning in Western Architecture*, p. 428.

3. See Husserl, *The Crisis of European Sciences...*

4. Compare the development of "thing constancy" in the child. Norberg-Schulz, *Intentions...* pp. 43ff.

5. M. Eliade, *Patterns in Comparative Religion*. Cleveland and New York 1963, p. 239,

6. Eliade, op. cit. p. 100.

7. K. Clark, *Landscape into Art*. London 1949, passim.

8. Eliade, op. cit. p. 269.

9. G. Bachelard, *The Poetics of Space*. New York 1964, p. 185.

10. Eliade, op. cit. p. 188.

11. op. cit. p. 269.

12. op. cit. p. 369.

13. Frankfort, op. cit. pp. 45, 51.

14. Ptahhotep, quoted after Frankfort, op. cit. p. 53.

15. Frankfort, op. cit. p. 54.

16. J. Trier, Irminsul, in *Westfälische Forschungen*, IV, 1941.

17. W. Müller, *Die heilige Stadt*. Stuttgart 1961, p. 16.

18. L. Curtius, *Die antike Kunst* II, 1. Die klassische Kunst Griechenlands. Potsdam 1938, pp. 15, 19.

19. V. Scully, *The Earth, the Temple and the Gods*. New Haven 1962, p. 9.

20. Scully, op. cit. p. 45.

21. O. Demus, *Byzantine Mosaic Decoration*. London 1948, p. 35.

22. Paradiso 31.22.

23. Clark, op. cit. p. 16.

24. W. Hellpach, *Geopsyche*. Stuttgart 1965 (1911).

25. It also gave rise to typical musical compositions such as *The Seasons* by Haydn.

26. The categories answer the questions, "What", "Where", "How", and "When".

27. Hellpach, op. cit. p. 192.

28. A. Sestini, *Il paesaggio*. Milano 1963, p. 92.

29. J. Gottmann, *A Geography of Europe*. London 1951, p. 265.

30. Finnish art is determined by these natural characters, as is particularly evident in the music of Sibelius.

31. Seen from the sea, the land in fact appears as a figure.

32. We can here only furnish a few indications.

33. In general it is necessary to consider the interaction of vegetation and surface relief.

34. Hellpach, op. cit. pp. 171ff.

35. Frankfort, op. cit. p. 47.

36. The silhouette is in fact of decisive importance in romantic landscape painting.

37. See J. Clay, *L'impressionisme*. Paris 1971, pp. 134ff.

38. With the exception of Venetian painting.

39. Norberg-Schulz, *Existence...* p. 21.

40. Cf. St. Francis' *Cantico delle creature*.

41. The seven traditional types of Japanese landscape are thus based on "strong" configurations of hills, plains, vegetation and water. See T. Haguchi, *The Visual and Spatial Structure of Landscape*. Tokyo 1975.

42. They also reappear in more recent literature, such as Ibsen's Peer Gynt.

43. It also implies an experience of the changing seasons.

44. For a most sensitive description of the character of the desert, see A. de St. Exupéry: *Citadelle*.

45. As for instance in Italian.

46. S.H. Nasr, *Sufi Essays*. London 1972, p. 51.

47. Nasr, op. cit. p. 88f., who refers to the Islamic image of the sky as the Divine throne (*al-'arsh*).

48. "Oasis" is an Egyptian word which means "dwelling place".

49. In the desert things as "destroyed" by light, in the North they become mysteriously luminous.

50. Curtius, op. cit. p. 15.

51. "Veduta" means something seen or looked at.

52. Rilke, IX Elegy.

III
MAN-MADE PLACE

1. The existential dimension of the man-made environment was intuited in the past, but is today reduced to the more superficial concept of "function".

2. Norberg-Schulz, *Intentions...*, p. 125.

3. G. von Kaschnitz-Weinberg, *Die eurasischen Grundlagen der antiken Kunst*. Frankfurt a.M. 1961.

4. This relationship is directly evident in the walls of Alatri in Latium.

5. Norberg-Schulz, *Meaning...*, chapter I.

6. G. von Kaschnitz-Weinberg, *Die mittelmeerischen Grundlagen der antiken Kunst*. Frankfurt a.M. 1944.

7. E. Baldwin Smith, *Egyptian Architecture as Cultural Expression*. New York and London 1938, p. 249.

8. Clark, op. cit. p. 10.

9. Kaschnitz-Weinberg, *Die mittelmeerischen...*, p. 55.

10. Trier, Irminsul. *Westfälische Forschungen*, IV, 1941. Trier, First. *Nachrichten von der Gesellschaft der Wissenschaften zu Göttingen*, phil.-hist. Klasse IV, NF III.4, 1940.

11. Thus Jaspers says, "In itself every existence appears round". K. Jaspers, *Von der Wahrheit*. München 1947, p. 50.

12. W. Müller, *Die heilige Stadt*. passim.

13. Müller, op. cit.

14. See chapter II of the present book.

15. Norberg-Schultz, *Meaning...* chapter II, passim.

16. As an example we may mention the architecture of Juvarra. See Norberg-Schulz, *Late Baroque and Rococo Architecture*. New York 1974.

17. Norberg-Schulz, *Meaning...*, p. 222.

18. D. Frey, *Grundlegung...*, p. 7.

19. The suburban dwelling also belongs to the category of "vernacular architecture".

20. Scully, *The Earth...*, p. 171.

21. Norberg-Schulz, *Meaning...*, pp. 77ff.

22. G. Nitschke, SHIME. *Architectural Design*, december 1974.

23. Nitschke, op. cit. p. 756.

24. Trier, First. pp. 86, 89.

25. R.J.C. Atkinson, *Stonehenge*. Harmondsworth 1960, pp. 22, 23, 56ff.

26. Portoghesi, *Le inibizioni...*

27. Norberg-Schulz, *On the Search for Lost Architecture*. Rome 1976, p. 40.

28. Le Corbusier, *Vers une Architecture*. Paris 1923.

29. Meitzen, *Siedlung und Agrarwesen der Westgermanen und Ostgermanen*. Berlin 1895.

30. As such it served the "open" space of American settlements.

31. See S. Bianca, *Architektur und Lebensform im islamischen Stadtwesen*. Zürich 1975.

32. Norberg-Schulz, *Late Baroque and Rococo Architecture*.

33. Venturi, *Complexity...*, p. 88.

34. Trier, First.

35. op. cit. pp. 22ff.

36. Heidegger, *Poetry...*, pp. 36, 45, 74.

37. In general see Scully, *The Earth, the Temple and the Gods*.

38. F.L. Wright, *The Natural House*. New York 1954, passim.

39. For a theory of building-tasks see Norberg-Schulz, *Intentions*, p. 151.

40. The names thus reflect our "image" of the city in terms of squares, streets and districts.

41. Cf. von Kaschnitz-Weinberg, *Die eurasischen Grundlagen...*

42. *Organhaft* should not be confused with "organic".

43. Romantic space, on the contrary, always "leads somewhere".

44. Bianca, op. cit.

45. Thus Vergil said: "When you comply with the gods, you are master".

46. We say "forms the basis for", because its identity is incomplete without a defined character.

47. See H.P. L'Orange, *Art Forms and Civic Life in the Late Roman Empire*. Princeton 1965.

48. Norberg-Schulz, *Meaning...*, pp. 250ff.

49. Le Corbusier, *Vers une Architecture*, English edition, London 1927, p. 31.

50. E. Panofsky, *Gothic Architecture and Scolasticism*. Latrobe 1951.

51. Norberg-Schulz, *Baroque Architecture*. New York 1971.

52. The Belvedere in Vienna stresses the romantic component, whereas the lay-out of Versailles is mainly of cosmic derivation.

53. Heidegger, *Die Kunst und der Raum*. St. Gallen 1969, pp. 9ff.

IV
PRAGUE

1. F. Kafka, Letter to Oskar Pollak 1902.

2. G. Meyrink, *Der Golem*. München 1969. Chapter "Spuk", pp. 121ff.

3. Menschen, die über dunkle Brücken gehn,
vorüber an Heiligen
mit matten Lichtlein.
Wolken, die über grauen Himmel ziehn
vorüber an Kirchen
mit verdämmernden Türmen.
Einer, der an der Quaderbrüstung lehnt
und in das Abendwasser schaut,
die Hände auf alten Steinen.

4. The word "cubist" is used in Prague to denote a particular local variant of early modern architecture, such as the works of Josef Gočár and Josef Chochol.

5. Only after the second World War the geographical and linguistic borders correspond.

6. The New Town had its own administration.

7. G. Fehr, *Benedikt Ried*. München 1961.

8. Norberg-Schulz, *Kilian Ignaz Dientzenhofer e il barocco boemo*. Rome 1968.

9. Goethe, Diary, 22. July 1806.

10. D. Libal, *Alte Städte in der Tschechoslowakei*. Prague 1971.

11. Norberg-Schulz, op. cit. pp. 85ff.

12. The project is probably by Kilian Ignaz Dientzenhofer, the execution by Anselm Lurago.

13. K.M. Swoboda, *Peter Parler*. Wien 1940.

14. Fehr, op. cit.

15. Norberg-Schulz, op. cit.

16. Norberg-Schulz, op. cit.

17. The same is the case in the Powder Tower.

18. Cf. Norberg-Schulz, *Meaning...*, p. 222.

19. Norberg-Schulz, Borromini e il barocco boemo, in *Studi sul Borromini*. Rome 1967. Norberg-Schulz, Lo spazio nell'architettura post-guariniana, in *Guarino Guarini e l'internazionalità del barocco*, Turin 1970.

20. E. Bachmann, Architektur, in *Barock in Böhmen* (ed. K.M. Swoboda), München 1964.

21. See Norberg-Schulz, *Kilian Ignaz Dientzenhofer...*

22. As in the works of Jan Kristofori.

23. G. Janouch, *Gespräche mit Kafka*. Frankfurt a.M. 1951, p. 42.

V
KHARTOUM

1. The Nile valley proper starts further to the north, at Sabaloka.

2. A first extension stems from 1912.

3. Cf. A. de St. Exupéry, *Citadelle*.

4. Bianca, *Architektur und Lebensform*.

5. *Living on the edge of the Sahara*, (Kasba 64 Study Group). The Hague 1973.

6. The colonnaded streets of Antiquity were usually transformed (built up) when they became Islamic. See Bianca: op. cit. p. 45.

7. Compare the desert settlements of the ancient Romans.

8. The early settlement at Soba on the Blue Nile only was of local importance.

9. By MEFIT S.p.A., Rome.

VI
ROME

1. E. Guidoni, Il significato urbanistico di Roma tra antichità e medioevo, in *Palladio XXII*, n. I-IV, 1972.

2. G. Kaschnitz von Weinberg, *Mittelmeerische Kunst*. Berlin 1965. H. Kähler, *Wandlungen der antiken Form*. München 1949.

3. H.P. L'Orange, *Romersk idyll*. Oslo 1952. A good general introduction to the character of Rome is offered by L. Quaroni, *Immagine di Roma*. Bari 1969.

4. L'Orange, op. cit. p. 17.

5. op. cit. p. 36.

6. op. cit. p. 8.

7. G. Lugli, *Il foro romano e il palatino*. Roma 1971, p. 102. Also J. Rykwert, *The Idea of a Town*. London 1976, p. 114.

8. Portoghesi, *Le inibizioni...*, p. 46ff.

9. Strangely enough, the Alban Hills have not yet been subject to a monographical study.

10. H. Kähler, Das Fortunaheiligtum von Palestrina Praeneste, in *Annales Universitatis Saraviensis*, vol. VII, no. 3-4, Saarbrücken 1958.

11. For the original topography of Rome see S. Muratori, R. Bollati, S. Bollati, G. Marinucci, *Studi per una operante storia urbana di Roma*. Roma 1963.

12. Guidoni, op. cit.

13. Guidoni, op. cit. p. 6. It is significant to note that Nero built his palace where the Colosseum now stands, expressing thus the wish for "taking possession" of the city.

14. Guidoni, op. cit. pp. 10ff. Guidoni points out that the churches of St. Peter and St. Paul were built far away from the places of their martyrdom, to make the symbolic cross possible.

15. See S. Giedion, *Space, Time and Architecture*. Cambridge, Mass. 1967, pp. 82ff.

16. Norberg-Schulz, *Meaning...*, p. 270.

17. Norberg-Schulz, *Baroque Architecture*.

18. Vergil, *Aeneid* VIII, 327-58.

19. Portoghesi, *Le inibizioni...*, pp. 44ff.

20. A. Boethius, *The Golden House of Nero*. Ann Arbor 1960, pp. 129ff.

21. Norberg-Schulz, *Meaning...*, pp. 119ff.

22. Borromini's Re Magi Chapel represents an exception.

23. Kaschnitz von Weinberg, *Mittelmeerische Kunst*, p. 513.

24. *The Odes of Horace*, Book I, IX.

25. Cf. Rykwert, op. cit.

26. We may in this context also remember the symmetrical *velarium* which was used to protect the spectators from the sun.

27. P.L. Nervi, *New Structures*. London 1963.

VII
PLACE

1. We may in this context remind of concepts such as "form" and "content".

2. Norberg-Schulz, *Intentions...* p. 43.

3. J. Piaget, *The Childs's Construction of Reality*. London 1955, pp. 88ff., pp. 209ff., pp. 350ff.

4. J. Piaget, *The Child's Conception of the World*. London 1929, p. 169.

5. Hellpach, *Geopsyche*.

6. G.W.F. Hegel, *Vorlesungen über die Philosophie der Geschichte*. Chapter on "Geographische Grundlagen der Weltgeschichte".

7. J.G. Herder, *Ideen zur Philosophie der Geschichte der Menschheit*. 7. Buch, III.

8. A. Toynbee, *A Study of History*.

9. It is doubtful, however, whether Marx himself

intended the one-sided approach of later Marxism. In his *Economic and Philosophical Manuscripts* from 1844 he understands man as an "artist" and as a "suffering being, and since he feels his suffering, a *passionate* being". See Marx, *Early Writings*, translated and edited by T.B. Bottomore. London 1963, pp. 206, 208.

10. Marx was the first to point out this danger in his *Economic and Philosophical Manuscripts*, ("Warenfetischismus").

11. Heidegger, *Poetry...*, pp. 172ff.

12. Norberg-Schulz, *Intentions...*, p. 74.

13. Cf. the Roman displacement of Egyptian obelisks etc., and the more recent importation of European works of art to the United States.

14. If they did, the place, the work of art etc. would become a mere ideological illustration.

15. Heidegger, pp. 149ff., op. cit.

16. Heidegger, op. cit. p. 151.

17. A. Rapoport, *House Form and Culture*, Englewood Cliffs 1969, turns these facts upside-down maintaining that the buildings of "the grand design tradition" are unusual and are built to "impress the populace"!

18. Heidegger, *Die Kunst und der Raum*, p. 13.

19. Heidegger, *Poetry...*, p. 43.

20. Heidegger, op. cit. p. 204.

21. Thus the Egyptians only built pyramids in the North. In the South, at Luxor-Thebes, they used the mountain itself.

22. The only large-scale exception is the desert, whose "cosmic" character in fact depends on the lack of particular directions. It is "isolated" and simultaneously "infinite".

23. See J.M. Houston, *A Social Geography of Europe*. London 1963. Chapter 8, pp. 157ff.

24. G. Bugge, C. Norberg-Schulz, *Early Wooden Architecture in Norway*. Oslo 1968.

25. In Italian the disposition is called "schema tentacolare".

26. For instance in the *Vierkanthof* or *Rundling*.

27. Heidegger, *Die Kunst und der Raum*, p. 11. My italics and quotation marks.

28. Giedion, *architecture you and me*. Cambridge, Mass. 1958, pp. 130ff.

29. Norberg-Schulz, Architekturornament, in *Ornament ohne Ornament* (m. Buchmann ed.), Zürich 1965.

30. Norberg-Schulz, *Intentions...* chapter on "Form".

31. Cf. the concept "strong Gestalt".

32. For variations on the *palazzo* and *hôtel* themes, see Norberg-Schulz, *Baroque Architecture*.

33. Norberg-Schulz, *Existence...*, p. 35. For a general discussion of alienation see R. Schacht, *Alienation*. New York 1970.

34. We ought to emphasize again that the atmosphere to a high extent depends on the conditions of *light*.

35. S. Kostof, *The Third Rome*. Berkeley 1973.

36. Designers Fazlur Kahn and Bruce Graham.

37. See *Boston Architecture* (D. Freeman ed.). Cambridge, Mass. 1970.

38. W.M. Whitehill, *Boston, a topographical History*. Boston 1968.

39. This has also been forgotten in a city such as Moscow.

40. A.N. Whitehead, *Process and Reality*. New York 1929, p. 515.

41. For instance in the works of Frank Lloyd Wright and in Scandinavian architecture.

42. L. Kahn, "Credo", in *Architectural Design*, 5/1974, p. 280.

43. Already Vitruvius wrote: "Southern peoples have the keenest wits, but lack valour, northern peoples have great courage but are slow-witted". VI, i, ii.

44. Cf. Karl Popper: *The Powerty of Historicism*. London 1961, pp. 64ff.

45. Giedion, *Constancy, Change and Architecture*. Harvard Univ. 1961.

46. Kahn, op. cit. p. 281.

47. Rilke, IX Elegy.
Preise dem Engel die Welt, nicht die unsägliche, *ihm*
kannst du nicht grosstun mit herrlich Erfühltem;
in Weltall
wo er fühlender fühlt, bist du ein Neuling. Drum zeig
ihm das Einfache, das, von Geschlecht zu Geschlechtern gestaltet,
als ein unsriges lebt, neben der Hand und im Blick.
Sag ihm die Dinge. Er wird staunender stehn; wie du standest
bei dem Seiler in Rom, oder beim Töpfer am Nil.
Zeig ihm, wie glücklich ein Ding sein kann, wie schuldlos und unser,
wie selbst das klagende Leid rein zu Gestalt sich entschliesst,
dient als ein Ding, oder stirbt in ein Ding – , und jenseits
selig der Geige entgeht. – Und diese, von Hingang
lebenden Dinge verstehn, dass du sie rühmest; vergänglich,
traun sie ein Rettendes uns, den Vergänglichsten zu.
Wollen, wir sollen sie ganz im unsichtbarn Herzen verwandeln
in – o unendlich – in uns! Wer wir am Ende auch seien.

VIII
PLACE TODAY

1. Kahn, *Credo*, p. 280.

2. Lynch, "The Image...", pp. 4-5.

3. A. Rapoport, R.E. Kantor, "Complexity and Ambiguity in Environmental Design", in *American Institute of Planners Journal*, July 1967.

4. See Chapter I of the present book.

5. Norberg-Schulz, "The Dwelling and the Modern Movement", in *LOTUS International*, no. 9, Milan 1975.

6. Le Corbusier, *La maison des hommes*. Paris 1942, p. 5.

7. Le Corbusier, *Vers une Architecture*, English edition, pp. 17ff.

8. Le Corbusier, *Vers...*, p. 268.

9. F.L. Wright, *The Natural House*, p. 15.

10. Wright, op. cit. p. 37.

11. Wright, op. cit. p. 51.

12. *Logement prolongé*.

13. Giedion, *architecture you and me*, passim.

14. P. Johnson, *Mies van der Rohe*. New York 1947.

15. Which, according to Le Corbusier are the *joies essentielles*.

16. H.R. Hitchcock, P. Johnson, *The International Style*. New York 1932.

17. W. Gropius, *The New Architecture and the Bauhaus*. London 1935, p. 18.

18. Gropius, op. cit. p. 20.

19. See for instance Lafayette Park in Detroit by Mies van der Rohe, 1955-63.

20. In P. Zucker, *New Architecture and City Planning*. New York 1944. Also in Giedion, *architecture you and me*, p. 28.

21. Giedion, op. cit. p. 127.

22. In *Architectural Record*, January 1954, "The State of Contemporary Architecture, the Regional Approach". Also in Giedion, op. cit. p. 145.

23. H. Berndt, A. Lorenzer, K. Horn, *Architektur als Ideologie*. Frankfurt a.M. 1968, p. 51.

24. Giedion, *Space, Time and Architecture*, p. 708.

25. Venturi, *Complexity and Contradiction in Architecture*. New York, 1966.

26. Giedion, *Space...* p. 620, pp. 645ff.
27. V. Scully, *Modern Architecture*. New York 1961, p. 45.
28. Le Corbusier, *Oeuvre complète 1946-52*. Zürich 1961, p. 72.
29. Scully, op. cit. p. 46. For an analysis see Norberg-Schulz, *Meaning...* pp. 407ff.
30. Scully, *Louis I. Kahn*. New York 1962, p. 36.
31. Louis I. Kahn, *L'architecture d'aujourd'hui 142*, Feb. 1969, p. 13.

32. Kahn, op. cit., p. 25.
33. Kahn, *Credo*.
34. Kahn, op. cit.
35. Heidegger, *Poetry...* p. 42.
36. Kahn, op. cit.
37. Scully, *Louis I. Kahn*, p. 33.
38. The term stems from S. Giedion.
39. A. Colquhoun, *Rational Architecture*, in "Architectural Design", June 1975.
40. We have in mind certain works by Rudolph, Yamasaki, Stone, Johnson, Kallmann etc. Cf. Giedion, *Napoleon and the Devaluation of Symbols*, in "Architectural Review", no. 11, 1947.
41. Giedion, *Space...* pp. 668ff.
42. Norberg-Schulz, *Meaning...* pp. 420ff.
43. C. Moore, D. Lyndon, *The Place of Houses*. New York 1975.
44. Giedion, *Constancy...* p. 7.
45. Giedion, *architecture you and me*. Cambridge, Mass 1958.

INDEX OF NAMES AND PLACES

Numbers in italics refer to illustrations

Aalto Alvar Hugo Henrik, Finnish architect, Kuortane 1898-1977, 70, 195, 196, 198, 200; *339, 340.*
Africa, 40, 116, 128; *185.*
Alatri, *289.*
Alban hills, 143, 146, 147, 149, 154, 164, 166; *31, 232, 239, 245.*
Albano, lake of, 67.
Alberti Leon Battista, Italian architect, Genoa 1406-Rome 1472, 58, 158, 166.
Alighieri Dante, 32.
Alps, 47.
America, 196.
Amiens, Cathedral, 86.
    Countryside, 70.
Antonio da Sangallo, the Younger (Antonio Cordini), Italian architect Florence 1483-Rome 1546, 157.
Anzio, 146.
    Temple of Fortune, 146.
Assisi, 173; *291, 292.*
    Eremo delle Carceri of St. Francis, 40; *60.*
Atelier 5, Swiss group of architects, 198.
Athens, the Acropolis, *121.*
    Propylaea, *120.*
    Temple of Nike, *122.*
Austria, 84, 108.

Bachelard Gaston, 25.
Baghdad, 122.
Bagnaia, 166.
Barbarano, 144.
    Forre, 231.
Barcelona, International Exposition, German pavilion, 194.
Bardonecchia, farmhouse, *110.*
B.B.P.R. (Banfi, Belgiojoso, Peressutti, Rogers), *348.*
Berlin, 21; *24.*
Berne, Siedlung Halen, 198.
Bernini Gian Lorenzo, Italian architect, Naples 1598-Rome 1680, 152, 164, 166; *251, 252, 273, 275.*
Bianco, Monte, *26.*
Birkehöj, 198.
Bofill Ricardo, Spanish architect, 200; *351.*
Bohemia, 84, 85, 97, 98, 99, 100, 104, 106, 108; *132.*
Bollnow O.F., 5, 21.
Bologna, *335.*

Bomarzo, 166.
Bořivoj, 85.
Borromini (Francesco Castelli), Italian architect, Bissone 1599-Rome 1667, 108, 153, 158, 163, 166; *265.*
Boston, 182; *312.*
    Baker House, *339.*
    Beacon Hill, 182.
    Copley Square, 182; *313.*
    John Hancock Tower, 182; *313.*
Brandenburg, 47.
Braun von Braun Matthias, *174.*
Brno, Tugendhat House, 195.

Calcata, *15.*
Calderini Guglielmo, Italian architect, Perugia 1837-Rome 1916, *330.*
Cambridge (Mass.), *309.*
    Massachusetts Avenue, *119.*
    M.I.T. Senior Dormitory, 196.
Caprarola, *97.*
Caratti Francesco, Italian architect, Bissone-Prague 1679, 106; *170.*
Castel d'Asso, 144.
Catalonia, 200.
Catanzaro (environs), S. Gregorio, olive grove, *34.*
Cavo, Monte, 146; *67, 232, 239.*
Celle, 70; *113.*
Ceské Budějovice, 99.
Cézanne Paul, *280.*
Chandigarh, Capitol, 197.
Charles IV, 85.
Charles, river, 182; *312, 339.*
Chia, *forre, 235.*
Chicago, 182.
    Federal Center, *333.*
    Robie House, *337, 338.*
    Sears Tower, 182; *311.*
Cimino, Monte, 147.
Civita Castellana, 144; *255.*
Cologne, 172.
Constantine, 150, 152, 161.
Constantinople, 152.
Corinth, Temple of Apollo, 66.
Cosenza (environs), S. Gregorio, *22.*
Curtius Ludwig, 45.
Czechoslovakia, 108.

Denmark, 34, 42, 58, 70; 142; *47, 58, 62.*
De Dominicis Anna Maria, 6.

Delphi, 31, 58.
    Temple of Apollo, 31; *38.*
    Tholos of Athena, 37.
    Theatre of Apollo, *38.*
Deyr el-Bahrī, Temple of Hasepsowe, *36.*
Dientzenhofer Cristoph, German architect, Aibling 1655-Prague 1722, 94, 98, 103, 104, 106, 108, 109; *143, 144, 153, 166, 172.*
Dientzenhofer Kilian Ignaz, German architect, Prague 1689-Prague 1751, 94, 100, 101, 102, 104, 106, 108, 109; *143, 153, 158, 160-162, 165, 168, 172.*
Dinkelsbühl, *112.*
Domažlice, 99.
Doxiadis Constantinos Apostolu, Greek architect, 120, 137; *194.*
Durrell Lawrence, 18.

Egypt, 24, 28, 116, 128.
Einbeck, *317.*
El Gizeh, temple of Chephren, *81.*
Eliade Mircea, 27.
England, 176.
Etiopia, 116.
Etruria, 143, 147, 148, 154, 164, 166.
Europe, 40, 42, 70, 84, 108, 171, 191, 192.

Finland, 35, 196.
Florence, 67, 172, 173; *286.*
    Ospedale degli Innocenti, *123.*
    Ponte Vecchio, *285.*
    Rucellai Palace, 158.
    Strozzi Palace, *109.*
Fischer von Erlach Johann Bernhard, Austrian architect and sculptor, Graz 1656-Vienna 1723, 102.
Forlì (environs), Marecchia valley, *41.*
France, 34, 35, 40, 200.
Frascati, 166.
Fredensborg, Dansk Samvirkes, 198.

Gerasa (Jordan) forum, *82.*
    Decumanus, *116.*
Germany, 70, 84, 194.
Giedion Siegfried, 12, 195, 198, 201.
Giglio, Castello, 175; *3, 293.*
    Giglio Porto, 175.
Goethe Johann Wolfgang, 18, 98, 166, 185.

Göllersdorf, Chapel, 2.
Göttweig, gateway to the abbey, 107.
Graham Ernest Robert, American architect, Lowell (Mich.) 1868-1936, 311.
Greece, 28, 45.
Gropius Walter, German architect, Berlin 1833-Boston 1970, 194.
Grosseto, 173.
Gualala (California), Sea Ranch, 350.
Guarini Guarino, Italian architect, Modena 1624-Milan 1683, 108.
Gubbio, 173.
Guidoni Enrico, 150.
Guimard Hector, French architect, Paris 1867-New York 1942, 329.

Harildstad, Heidal, 284.
Häring Hugo, 70, 71.
Hawksmoor Nicholas, English architect, Ragnall 1661-London 1736, 12, 306.
Hegel Georg Wilhelm Friedrich, 168, 185.
Heidegger Martin, 5, 6, 8, 10, 12, 13, 15, 18, 21, 22, 23, 65, 165, 168, 169, 170, 176, 198.
Hellpach Willy, 32.
Helsingör, Kingo houses, 198.
Herder Johann Gottfried, von, 168.
Hesiod, 24.
Hesse Hermann, 21.
Hildebrandt Johann Lucas von, German architect, Genoa 1668-Vienna 1745, 100; 2, 305.
Hofstadter A., 5.
Hölderlin Friedrich, 23.
Holland, 40.
Horace, 164.
Hus Jan, 108.

Ibrahim Ibn' Jakub, 85.
Iceland, 53.
Idria, valley of (Puglia), 42.
In der Wies, sanctuary, 99.
Innsbruck, 70; 105.
Ireland, 53.
Isernia, Capracotta, 8.
Islam, 45, 116, 135, 136.
Istanbul, courtyard of the Mirimah mosque, 117.
Italy, 40, 70, 173; 46, 61.

Japan, 58.
Jenney William Le Baron, American architect, Fairhaven (Mass.) 1832-Los Angeles 1907, 182.
Jičin, 99.

Kafka Franz, 5, 78, 82, 108.
Kähler H., 140.
Kahn Louis, American architect, Osel Island (Estonia) 1901-New York 1974, 6, 18, 184, 185, 197, 198, 200; 311, 344-346.
Kallmann Gerhard, 21.
Kaschnitz von Weinberg G., 140, 164.
Khartoum (Sudan), 113-138, 170, 179, 180; 21, 33, 177, 187-189, 195, 196, 198, 206, 212, 214-217.
    Abu Said, 118.
    Fallata, 226.
    Grand Hotel, 134.
    Great Mosque, 122; 197.
    Halfaya, 118.
    Hamad, 118.
    Khogali, 118, 120, 136; 191, 192.
    Khogali Mosque, 125; 224.
    Khogali Tomb, 126, 136; 224.
    Lord Kitchener's Palace, 122, 134; 222, 223.
    Moqren, 118.
    Railway Station, 122.
    Suk, 114; 181, 213.
    Tuti island, 113, 114, 118, 120, 124, 136; 177, 190, 215.
    — Village, 118.
    University (formerly Gordon College), 124, 134.
    — Faculty of Medicine, 122.
    Streets:
    —El Gamhuriya, 122.
    —El Gamia, 124.
    —El Kalifa-El Gami, 122; 198.
    —El Qasr, 122.
    War Memorial, 122.
    (environs), forest of Sunt, 115.
    (environs), village, 5.
Kitchener Horatio Herbert, 113, 120, 122, 131, 133, 134, 137; 196.
Kleivi, Aamotsdal, loft, 103.
Kloster Banz, 302.

Labe (Elbe), 84.
Langer Susanne, 23.
Lanuvio, 239.
    Temple of Imo, 146.
La Perthus (Catalonia), 351.
Lazio (Latium), 142, 146, 149, 166; 234.

Le Corbusier (Charles-Edouard Jeanneret), French architect, La Chaux-de-Fonds 1887-Cap Martin 1965, 6, 61, 76, 191, 192, 194, 196, 197, 198, 200; 334, 335, 341-343.
Lepine mountains, 147.
Liguria, 34.
Litomyšl, 99.
London, 172.
    St. George in the East, 306.
    St. Mary's Woolnoth, 12.
L'Orange H.P., 140.
Lorenzer Alfred, 195.
Lucca, 173.
    ENPAS building, 347.
Lüneburger Heide, 55.
Lurago Anselmo Martino, Italian architect, Como 1702 c.-Prague 1765, 165.
Luxor, oasis, 66.
    Temple of Amenophis III, 80.
Lynch Kevin, 12, 19, 20, 190, 201.

Mahdi, 137.
Malta, megalithic temples, 52.
Mantua, church of S. Andrea, 166.
Maratea (Potenza), 51.
Marseilles, Unité d'Habitation, 196.
Marx Karl, 168.
Mathey Jean-Baptiste, French architect and painter Dijon 1630-Paris 1695, 102, 108.
Mecca, 40.
Meger, 40.
Mengoni Giuseppe, Fontanelice (Bologna) 1829-Milan 1877, 328.
Meyrink Gustav, 78.
Michelangelo Buonarroti, Caprese (Arezzo) 1475-Rome 1564, 108, 151, 153, 166; 249, 250, 264, 268, 278.
Michigan, lake 182.
Mies van der Rohe Ludwig, German architect, Aachen 1886-Chicago 1972, 66, 182, 194, 195; 333.
Milan, Galleria Vittorio Emanuele, 328.
    Piazza Meda, office building, 348.
Morocco, 118.
M.L.T.W. (Moore, Lyndon, Thurnbull, Witaker). 200; 350.
Monet Claude, 40.
Monferrato, 34; 48.
Montagnana, 173; 288.
Montepulciano, stone building, 104.

Monteriggioni, *25, 91, 279.*
Moscow, *287, 331.*
    Kremlin, 173.

Naples, 47; *23, 71, 316.*
Nemi, lake, 146; *232, 239.*
Nepi, 144.
Neresheim, *13.*
    Monastery, *13.*
Nervi Pier Luigi, Italian architect, Sondrio 1891-Rome 1979, 166.
Neumann Johann Balthasar, German architect, Eger (Bohemia) 1687-Würzburg 1753, *13, 302.*
New York, World's Fair, Finnish pavilion, 195.
Nile, 28, 52, 115, 116, 118, 122, 125, 126, 135; *184, 205.*
    Blue Nile, 113, 114, 116, 118, 125, 131, 136, 137; *188, 216.*
    White Nile, 113, 114, 115, 116, 118, 125, 136, 137; *179, 225.*
Nitschke Günter, 58.
Noormarkku, Villa Mairea, 196; *340.*
Norchia, 144, 155.
    Forre, 238.
Norway, 40, 42, 70, 172; *44, 52, 101.*
Nové Město nad Mctuji, 99.

Olympia, 58.
Omdurman, 113, 114, 116, 118, 120, 125, 130, 133, 135, 136, 137; *180, 195, 200-203, 207, 210, 211, 218, 219.*
    Mahdi Square, 125.
    Quarters:
    — Abu Rouf, 120.
    — Beit El Mal, 120.
    Suk, 114, 125, 133; *218, 219.*
    Tomb of the Mahdi, *135.*
Orvieto, 173.
Oslo, 40; *327.*
    National Gallery, *280.*
    (environs), forest, *4.*
Ostia, 158; *299.*
Ostuni, 98.
Otaniemi (Helsinki), Finnish Student's Union Building, *349.*

Paestum, Temple of Hera, 66.
    Temple of Hera II, *83.*

Palermo, Cappella Palatina, *85.*
    S. Cataldo, *92.*
Palestine, 45.
Palestrina, 143, 147, 148, 165; *233, 242.*
    Temple of Fortuna Primigenia, 147; *241, 242.*
Palladio Andrea, Italian architect, Padua 1508-Maser 1580, 106.
Palo Alto (California), Hanna House, *336.*
Palombara Sabina, 173; *96.*
Paris, 172; *108, 304.*
    Castel Béranger, *329.*
    Exposition Internationale des Arts Décoratifs, 191.
    — Pavilion of Esprit Nouveau, 191; *335.*
    Guimard's house, *115.*
Parler Peter, Swabian architect, Prague 1325-1399, 98, 102, 104; *149.*
Pei Jeoh Ming, Chinese architect, Canton (China) 1917, 182; *313.*
Peking, Temple of Heaven, *100.*
Peruzzi Baldassarre, Italian architect, 1481-1536, *263.*
Petra (Jordan), *17, 28, 30, 79.*
Philadelphia, Richards Medical Research Building, *346.*
Piaget Jean, 13, 20, 180.
Pietilä Reima, Finnish architect, 1923, 200; *349.*
Pisticci (Basilicata), *95.*
Pitigliano, *88.*
Po valley, *310.*
Poissy, Ville Savoye (by Le Corbusier), 194.
Poland, 84.
Portoghesi Paolo, Italian architect, 12, 59, 155; *347.*
Prague, 78-110, 170, 180; *126, 127, 129, 131, 133, 135, 139, 148, 150, 175, 176.*
    Bridges:
    — Charles, 82, 85, 86, 92, 97; *130, 140, 141.*
    — Judith, 86.
    Casino of the Belvedere, 106; *171.*
    Churches:
    — Brevnov, 103, 104; *166, 167.*
    — Holy Vergin, 85.
    — St. John on the Rock, 104; *168, 169.*
    — St. Nicholas (in the Old Town), 87, 101, 102, 109; *162-164.*
    — St. Nicholas (in the Small Town), 81, 94, 103, 109; *142-146, 153.*
    — Týn, 81, 86, 96, 102; *128.*
    Hradčany, 78, 81, 85, 87, 94.
    — Castle, 81, 85, 86, 87; *134, 147.*
    — — Vladislav Hall, 94, 103, 104, 106; *152.*
    — Letna Park, 85.
    — Petřin Park, 85; *147.*

    — Square, 87.
Loreto Sanctuary, *172.*
New Town (Nové Město), 85, 87, 94, 97.
Old Town (Staré Město), 78, 81, 82, 85, 86, 87, 92, 94, 97, 101, 104.
    — Durchhaus, 92; *159.*
    — Ghetto, 85, 109.
    — Old Town Square (Staroměstské Náměstí), 86, 94, 101; *138.*
    — St. Venceslaus Square (Vaclavské Náměsti), 87.
Palaces:
    — Clam-Gallas, 102.
    — Czernin, 106; *170.*
    — Kinsky, 102; *165.*
    — of the Old Town, *158.*
    — Thun-Hohenstein, *174.*
    — Toscana, 102.
    — Town Hall, 86, 87.
Small Town (Málá Strana), 81, 82, 85, 86, 87, 92, 94, 103; *134, 151, 157.*
    — Small Town Square (Malostranské Naměti), 86; *145, 156.*
Streets:
    — Celetná, 86.
    — Mostecká, 87, 94; *142.*
    — Nerudová, 87, 94.
St. Vitus Cathedral, 81, 87, 94, 102, 104; *147, 149.*
St. Vitus Hill, 94.
Towers:
    — Powder, 86; *136.*
    — Bridge, 106.
    Týn, 86.
    — Courtyard, *137.*
Vyšehrad, fortress, 78, 94.
(environs), Smichov, Portheimka by Kilian Ignaz Dientzenhofer, 100; *160, 161.*
Priene (Asia Minor), 58; *90, 318.*
Procida, *308.*
Prussia, 84.

Rajhrad (Moravia), church, *173.*
Rapoport, 5.
Ratisbon, 172.
Ried Benedikt, Czech architect, Prague 1454-1534, 94, 103; *152.*
Rilke Rainer Maria, 6, 15, 48, 185.
Rochester (N.Y.), Unitarian Church, *344, 345.*
Roesler Franz, *228.*
Rome, 28, 98, 136, 138-166, 170, 173, 180; *227, 243, 246, 258, 277.*
    Campo Marzio, 148, 157.

Capitol (Campidoglio) 154, 161.
Capitoline hill 148, 154.
Churches (and basilicas):
— Constantine, *253.*
— Maxentius, 164.
— St. Agnes's, 164.
— S. Andrea della Valle, *270.*
— S. Carlo alle Quattro Fontane (St. Carlino's) 163; *271.*
— S. Costanza, *269.*
— St. John's in the Lateran, 150, 163.
— S. Ivo, 153.
— St. Paul's, 150.
— St. Peter's, 150, 153, 161; *278.*
— S. Sabina, *89.*
Colosseum, 150, 151, 152, 160, 165, 166; *266.*
Janiculus hill, 148.
Jewish Ghetto, *259.*
Palatine hill 143, 148, 149.
Palazzi:
— Cancelleria, 158; *262.*
— Conservatori, *268.*
— Farnese, 158; *264.*
— — courtyard, *267.*
— Giustizia, *330.*
— Massimo, *263.*
— Propaganda Fide, 158; *265.*
— Sport, 166.
— Vidoni, *84.*
Pantheon, 52, 153, 161, 164, 165; *254.*
Squares:
— Capitoline, 151, 152, 160; *249, 250.*
— del Popolo, 151; *248.*
— Navona, 155, 164; *229, 272, 273.*
— S. Pietro, 152, 160, 161, 164; *251, 252, 275.*
Temple of Jupiter, 149.
Temple of Venus and Rome, 150.
Trastevere, 148, 157.
Trevi fountain, *276.*
Spanish Steps, *274.*
Streets:
— Biberatica, 158; *260.*
— Governo Vecchio, *261.*
— Sacra, 149; *245.*
— Vittorio Emanuele, 180.
Trajan's forum, Via Biberatica, *260.*
Vatican, 150.
Vatican Circus, 150.
Romagna, 43.
Ronchamp, Ste. Marie-du-Haut, 196; *341-343.*
Rossi Aldo, Italian architect, Milan 1931, 198.
Rothenburg, *300.*

Sacco valley, 147; *230.*
Saint-Dié, 197.

Salerno, *303.*
Salzburg, 18.
Sangallo Antonio, the Younger, Italian architect, Florence 1483 - Rome 1546, 158; *264.*
San Gimignano, *10, 94.*
San Giuliano (Viterbo), *256.*
Santin Aichel Johann, architect of Italian origin, Prague 1667-1723, 108; *173, 174.*
Saqqāra, step pyramid, *78.*
Saxony, 84.
Säynätsalo, Town Hall, 196.
Scandinavia, 40, 42; *59.*
Scully Vincent, 197.
Segni (Lazio), megalithic structure, *77.*
Selinunte, temple, *106.*
Serlio Sebastiano, Italian architect, Bologna 1475 - Fontainebleau 1555, 54, 157.
Sermoneta, *11.*
Setesdal, valley, 172.
Siena, 67, 173, 176; *111, 290.*
    Cathedral Square, 176.
    Il Campo, *9, 93.*
    Town Hall, 176.
Sixtus V, 151; *247.*
SOM (Khan, Graham), 182; *311.*
Soracte, Mount, 147, 164; *240.*
    Temple of Soranus, 147.
Soriano al Cimino, 69.
Sperlonga, 175; *294.*
Stirling James, English architect, 200.
Stonehenge, 58.
Strasbourg, Cathedral, *124.*
Subiaco (environs), Speco of St. Benedict, 40; *7, 39.*
    (environs), valley, 56.
Sudan, 113, 116, 118, 136, 137; *315.*
Sutri, 144.
Sweden, 40, 198.
Switzerland, 84.
Sydney, Opera House, 198.

Telč, 109.
Telemark, old cottage, *6.*
    Cottage, *314.*
    Valley, 172.
Tiber, 143, 144, 147, 148, 150.
Tivoli, 146, 166.
Tjønntveit, lofts, *114.*
Toynbee Arnold, 168.
Trakl Georg, 8, 9, 10, 13, 23, 69.

Třebon, popular Baroque houses, *155.*
Tunis, clay houses, *102.*
Turin, 172.
Tuscany, 34.
Tusculum, 146.
Tuti, island of, s. Khartoum.

Ukraine, 84.
Urnes (Norway), Stave church, *76.*
United States, 198; *332.*
Utzon, Jörn, Danish architect, Copenaghen 1918, 198.

Valdarno, 46.
Vaux-le-Vicomte, Baroque garden palace, *125.*
Veio, Etruscan tomb, *237.*
    Brook, *35.*
Velletri, Palazzo Comunale, *301.*
Venice, 47; *73.*
    S. Giorgio Maggiore, *298.*
    St. Mark's square, 176; *295-297.*
Venturi Robert, American architect, 14, 15, 63, 194, 195, 201.
Vergil, 154, 161.
Versailles, 194.
Vesuvio, *27, 72.*
Vienna Belvedere, 100, 106; *87, 305.*
Vitorchiano, 144; *236, 257.*
    Ravine, *50.*
Vitruvius, Roman architect, I cnt. B.C., 54.
Vltava, 81, 84, 85, 99; *129.*

Whitehead Alfred North, 182.
Wright Frank Lloyd, American architect, Richlan Center 1869 - Phoenix 1959, 67, 192, 194, 196; *336-338.*

Yemen, 118.

Zurich, *19.*
    Theatre, 198.

SOURCES OF ILLUSTRATIONS

Alifoto, Rome: 249.
Alinari, Florence: 84, 264, 267.
Aurelio Amendola, Pistoia: 92.
Bruno Balestrini, Milan: 37, 78, 83, 86, 89.
Bildarchiv Foto Marburg, Marburg Lahn: 130, 149.
Brandaglia, Isola del Giglio: 293.
Deutsches Archaeologisches Institut, Rome: 269.
Jan Digerud, Oslo: 344.
John Ebstel: 345.
Robert Emmett Bright, Rome: 250.
ENIT, Rome: 8, 14, 22, 34, 41, 42, 43, 51, 68, 71, 72, 256, 290.
Fotocielo, Rome: 91, 96, 97, 98, 232, 233, 239, 248, 279, 288, 295.

Gavlas, Prague: 131.
Giuliano Gresleri, Bologna: 335.
Hedrich-Blessing, Chicago: 311, 333.
Jaatinen, Helsinki: 349.
Lucien Hervé, Neuilly-sur-Seine: 341, 342.
Pepi Merisio, Bergamo: 252, 268, 270, 271, 274, 275, 276, 277, 278.
Christian Norberg-Schulz, Oslo: 1, 2, 3, 4, 5, 7, 9, 10, 11, 12, 13, 15, 16, 17, 21, 23, 24, 25, 27, 28, 29, 30, 31, 32, 33, 35, 36, 39, 46, 47, 50, 55, 56, 57, 58, 62, 63, 64, 65, 66, 67, 69, 70, 73, 74, 75, 79, 80, 81, 82, 85, 87, 93, 99, 101, 102, 103, 105, 106, 107, 108, 110, 112, 113, 114, 115, 116, 117, 118, 119, 120, 121, 122, 123, 128, 129, 137, 138, 139, 140, 141, 142, 143, 144, 145, 146, 151, 153,

155, 156, 157, 158, 159, 160, 161, 162, 163, 164, 165, 166, 167, 170, 171, 172, 173, 174, 175, 179, 180, 181, 182, 183, 188, 189, 190, 191, 192, 193, 194, 199, 200, 201, 202, 203, 204, 205, 206, 207, 208, 209, 210, 211, 213, 214, 215, 216, 217, 218, 219, 220, 221, 222, 223, 224, 225, 226, 229, 230, 231, 236, 237, 238, 240, 241, 242, 245, 251, 255, 257, 259, 260, 261, 262, 263, 265, 266, 268, 272, 273, 284, 285, 286, 289, 291, 292, 297, 298, 299, 302, 303, 304, 305, 306, 309, 310, 312, 313, 314, 315, 316, 317, 328, 329, 330, 343, 346, 348.
A. Paul, Prague: 168, 169.
Paolo Portoghesi, Rome: 26, 48, 77, 88, 94, 104, 109, 111, 177, 187, 212, 235, 294, 301, 347.
Ivor Smith, Bristol: 307.
Wideröe, Oslo: 40, 52, 53, 54.

CONTENTS

PREFACE		5
Chapter one	PLACE?	6
Chapter two	NATURAL PLACE	23
Chapter three	MAN-MADE PLACE	50
Chapter four	PRAGUE	78
Chapter five	KHARTOUM	113

Chapter six	ROME	138
Chapter seven	PLACE	166
Chapter eight	PLACE TODAY	189
NOTES		203
INDEX OF NAMES AND PLACES		209
SOURCES OF ILLUSTRATIONS		213